NOW YOU KNOW

KNOW

SOCCER

NOW YOU KNOW

KNOW

SOCCER

Doug Lennox

DUNDURN PRESS
TORONTO

Editor: Shaun Smith
Copy-Editor: Shannon Whibbs
Design: Courtney Horner
Printer: Webcom

Library and Archives Canada Cataloguing in Publication

Lennox, Doug
    Now you know soccer / by Doug Lennox.

Includes index.
ISBN 978-1-55488-416-2

    1. Soccer--Miscellanea. I. Title.

GV943.2.L45 2009   796.33402   C2009-900499-2

1   2   3   4   5   13   12   11   10   09

Conseil des Arts   Canada Council
du Canada   for the Arts

Canadä

ONTARIO ARTS COUNCIL
CONSEIL DES ARTS DE L'ONTARIO

We acknowledge the support of **The Canada Council for the Arts** and the **Ontario Arts Council** for our publishing program. We also acknowledge the financial support of the **Government of Canada** through the **Book Publishing Industry Development Program** and **The Association for the Export of Canadian Books**, and the **Government of Ontario** through the **Ontario Book Publishers Tax Credit program**, and the **Ontario Media Development Corporation**.

Care has been taken to trace the ownership of copyright material used in this book. The author and the publisher welcome any information enabling them to rectify any references or credits in subsequent editions.

J. Kirk Howard, President

Printed and bound in Canada.
Printed on recycled paper.

www.dundurn.com

Dundurn Press
3 Church Street, Suite 500
Toronto, Ontario, Canada
M5E 1M2

Gazelle Book Services Limited
White Cross Mills
High Town, Lancaster, England
LA1 4XS

Dundurn Press
2250 Military Road
Tonawanda, NY
U.S.A. 14150

contents

preface

In July 2007 the world governing body of soccer, FIFA (*Fédération Internationale de Football Association*), released the results of a major multi-year survey of its member nations called "The Big Count." What was the big news they discovered with their fancy survey? Only that soccer is the most popular game in the world. Which of course begs the question, did they really need to ask?

Everyone with a piece of ground and a ball can start playing soccer. Maybe that is why it is called "the beautiful game," because of its tremendous egalitarian qualities. Rich or poor, it really doesn't matter on the soccer pitch, or the cobblestone street, or the patch of desert sand. Soccer has a way of equalizing things.

Soccer has also been called "the simplest game" and that is deceptive, for at its best it is a game of tremendous skill and awesome athleticism. It is also a game of remarkable power, which can mold cultures and shape lives. It can make us scream with delight, or cry with outrage — whether we're running down the touchline ourselves, just barely in control of the ball, or watching a master on TV who seems like he must have wings on his heels.

Over 265 million people, the FIFA study informs us, are actively involved in soccer around the world today. I've tried my best to provide a cross-section of that world in this book, packing it with questions and queries, lists and facts, anecdotes and answers. Soccer is indeed both beautiful and simple, and I hope that while reading this book, you'll share my feeling that through those two traits, it has also become the world's most fascinating game.

grass roots

What is the origin of soccer?

Soccer-like games that involved the kicking of a ball across a playing pitch have existed for eons in regions from China to Meso-America to the Arctic tundra. But modern soccer, as it evolved in Great Britain, has its roots in a medieval European game called "mob football," which was played between rival villages at times of celebration and festivity, especially on Shrove Tuesday. Played in England, Normandy, Brittany, Picardy, Cornwall, Wales, Scotland, and Ireland, mob football saw teams of unlimited size trying to force a ball (often an inflated pig's bladder) into an opponent village's main square or onto its church's steps. The rules were vague and play was often extremely violent, leading to broken limbs, internal injuries, and even the occasional death.

Quickies
Did you know ...
- the first recorded soccer death was in 1280 when in a game of mob football at Ulgham, near Ashington in Northumberland, a player was killed as a result of running against an opposing player's sheathed dagger?

Why did both Edward II and Edward III both prohibit soccer?

Some Bluebloods Who Banned Soccer
- Edward II of England, in 1314
- Phillippe V of France, in 1319
- Edward III of England, in 1349
- Charles V of France, in 1369
- James I of Scotland, in 1424
- James II of Scotland, in 1457
- Henry VII of England, in 1540

In 1314 King Edward II issued a prohibition against so called "mob football" because of the chaotic impact that "this hustling over large balls" had on the city life in London. Edward III also prohibited "futeball" in 1349 because it distracted able-bodied men from archery practice.

Who owned the first pair of football boots?

King Henry VIII's soccer shoes — called football boots — were listed within the Great Wardrobe of 1526, a shopping list of the day. They were made by his personal shoemaker, Cornelius Johnson, in 1525, at a cost of

4 shillings, the modern equivalent of CDN$160 (US$127). Little is known about them, as there is no surviving example, but the royal football boots are known to have been made of strong leather, ankle-high, and heavier than the normal shoe of the day.

What British king was first to give soccer royal approval?

Charles II of England gave the game of soccer royal approval in 1681 when he attended a match between the Royal Household and the Duke of Albemarle's servants.

What was *tsu chu*?

As far back as 2500 BC a game of kicking a ball called *tsu chu* (also spelled as *cuju*) was played in China. *Tsu* means "to kick the ball with feet" and *chu* means "a ball made of leather and stuffed." Matches were often staged in celebration of the emperor's birthday. The objective was for players to kick a ball through a round opening into a small net attached to bamboo poles. The opening was about 1 foot (30–40 centimetres) wide and elevated about 30 feet (nine metres) from the ground. During the Ts'in Dynasty (255 BC–206 BC) a form of *tsu chu* was used for training by soldiers, and from the Han Dynasty (206 BC–220 AD) there survives a war manual featuring physical exercises called *tsu chu*. These exercises involved a leather ball filled with feathers and hair. With the exception of the hands, all other body parts could be used while trying to "score."

> **Quickies**
> *Did you know ...*
> • the first instance of the modern spelling of "football" appeared in 1608, in act 1, scene 4 of Shakespeare's *King Lear*: "Nor tripped neither, you base football player"?

What was *kemari*?

Between 300 AD–600 AD a game called *kemari* emerged in Japan. Also called *kenatt*, it was played by eight or fewer people using a sawdust-stuffed deerskin ball about 9 inches (22 centimetres) in diameter. On a rectangular field called a *kikytsubo*, players had to juggle the ball with their feet and pass it to one another in the air, keeping it from touching the ground. Each corner of the *kikytsubo* was marked with a sapling, the classic version featuring a cherry, maple, willow, and pine. When kicking the ball up, a player would call "*ariyaaa!*" (here we go) and when passing it to someone else, "*ari!*" (here). The golden age for *kemari* was between the tenth and sixteenth centuries, as the game spread to the lower classes and became a popular subject for poets. One surviving anecdote tells of an emperor and his team who kept the ball aloft for over 1,000 kicks. Beginning in the thirteenth century, *kemari* players wore uniforms based on the traditional samurai's costume, the *hitatare*.

Quickies
Did you know ...
• an ancient Greek marble relief housed in the National Museum of Archeology in Athens shows an athlete balancing a ball on his thigh as a young boy looks on? This very same image is featured on the European Cup trophy.

What was *episkyros*?

Around 2000 BC, the Greeks played *episkyros* (also known as *phaininda*), a kicking and throwing game played primarily by men, usually in the nude. Early balls were made of linen and hair wrapped in string and sewn together, though it is believed inflated balls — inflated pig bladders wrapped in pigskin or deerskin — were used by later practitioners of the game.

Quickies
Did you know ...
• Cicero describes an incident in which a man getting a open-air shave was killed when a *harpastum* ball hit his barber?

What was *harpastum*?

For over 700 years during the realm of the Roman Empire, a game called *harpastum* (meaning "the small ball game") was very popular. Employing a small, hard ball, *harpastum* was played by 5–12 athletes on a rectangular pitch marked by boundary lines and split by a centre line. The game's objective seems thoroughly counterintuitive to us today: each team had to keep the ball in their own half for as long as they could, while their opponents tried to steal it and take to their side. Both the hands and feet could be used to move the ball. Because the rules indicated that only the player with the ball could be tackled, complex passing combinations developed. Emperor Julius Caesar used *harpastum* to maintain the physical readiness of his soldiers.

> **Quickies**
> *Did you know ...*
> • there are records of a *harpastum* match being played between the Romans and the British natives?

What was *pok-a-tok*?

As far back as 3000 BC, Mayans and other inhabitants of the Meso-American region played a game called *pok-a-tok*, in which the ball could only be touched with the elbows, hips or knees. The exceedingly challenging objective was to project the ball through a ring attached to a sloping wall.

> **Quickies**
> *Did you know ...*
> • the Inuit played a game called *asqaqtuk*, which involved booting a heavy ball stuffed with grass, caribou hair, and moss across the arctic tundra between goals as much as 10 miles (16 kilometres) apart?

What was *pasuckuakohowog*?

North American Indians played a soccer-like game called *pasuckuakoho-wog*, which means "they gather to play ball with the foot." It was played in the early 1600s on beaches along the Massachusetts coast with half-mile-wide goals about one mile apart. As many as 1,000 players dressed in disguise and with war paint on their faces participated in these rather violent games, which went on for several days and ended with a feast.

Why is Piazza della Novere in Florence considered by some to be the cradle of European soccer?

In the sixteenth-century in Florence, Italy, there emerged an early European cousin of soccer called *calcio*. It was played in the city's Piazza della Novere by teams of 27 using the feet and hands to try to kick, throw, or carry a ball over a designated spot on the perimeter of a playing pitch covered in sand. The first official rules of *calcio* were published in 1580 AD by Giovanni Bardi. Originally, *calcio* was only reserved for the rich aristocrats, who played every night between Epiphany and Lent.

What is the oldest record of a soccer club in existence?

The title of the world's oldest soccer club is often disputed, or is claimed by several different clubs, across several different codes of soccer. It is possible that an organization of soccer players existed in London between 1421 and 1423. The records of the Brewers' Company of London, a guild, mention the hiring out of their hall "by the 'ffooteballepleyers' for 20 pence," under the heading "Trades and Fraternities." The listing of such players as a "fraternity" is the earliest allusion to what might be considered a soccer club.

Quickies

Did you know ...

• on February 17, 1530, while the troops of Charles V, Holy Roman Emperor, were besieging Florence, a game of *calcio* was organized in the city as a show of defiance?

What is the oldest national soccer team in the world?

That would be a tie. Both Scotland and England were the first countries to put forward national teams in 1872. In fact, they did so for a match against each other, which also allows them to share the credit of holding the first international match. The game was held at Hamilton Crescent in Partick, Scotland, on November 30 that year, and, appropriately enough, it ended in a goal-less tie.

Who drew up the first set of soccer rules?

During the eighteenth century, the game of mob football evolved into a codified sport at England's public schools like Eton, Westminster, Rugby, Charterhouse, and Harrow. The first-ever set of formal soccer rules were written at Eton College in 1815, though each school tended to have their own set of rules.

What is the world's oldest soccer club?

The Sheffield Football Club was founded in 1857 in Sheffield by Nathaniel Creswick and William Prest, and is now recognized as the world's oldest club. The club initially played its own code of football: the Sheffield rules. Players were allowed to push or hit the ball with their hands, and there was no offside rule at all, so that players known as "kick throughs" could be permanently positioned near the opponents' goal.

What are the Cambridge Rules?

In 1848, representatives from Eton, Harrow, Rugby, Winchester, and Shrewsbury schools gathered at Trinity College, at Cambridge University, for a meeting to codify the rules of soccer. These were the first set of rules to be used collectively by multiple school teams. When the country's leading clubs and schools got together to form the Football Association in 1863, they used the Cambridge Rules as the basis for a new set of FA rules.

The Cambridge Rules as of November 1863

Rule 1: The length of the ground shall be not more than 150 yards (137 metres). The ground shall be marked out by posts, and two posts shall be placed on each side line, at a distance of 25 yards (23 metres) from each goal line.

Rule 2: The goals shall consist of two upright poles at a distance of 15 feet (4.5 metres) from each other.

Rule 3: The choice of goals and kickoff shall be determined by tossing, and the ball shall be kicked off from the middle of the ground.

Rule 4: In a match when half the time agreed upon has elapsed, the sides shall change goals when the ball is next out of play. After a change or a goal is obtained, the kickoff shall be from the middle of the ground in the same direction as before. The time during which the match shall last and the numbers on each side are to be settled by the heads of the sides.

Rule 5: When a player has kicked the ball, anyone of the same side who is nearer to the opponent's goal line is out of play, and may not touch the ball himself, nor may in any way whatsoever prevent any other player from doing so.

Rule 6: When the ball goes out of the ground by crossing the sidelines, it is out of play, and shall be kicked straight into the ground again from the point it is first stopped.

Rule 7: When a player has kicked the ball beyond the opponent's goal line; whoever first touches the ball (touchdown) when it is on the ground with his hands may have a free kick, bringing the ball 25 yards (23 metres) straight out from the goal line.

Rule 8: No player may touch the ball behind his opponent's goal line; who is behind it when the ball is kicked there.

Rule 9: If the ball is touched down behind the goal line and beyond the line of the side posts, the free kick shall be from the 25-yard (22.8-metre) post.

Rule 10: When a player has a free kick, no one of his own side may be between him and his opponent's goal line, and no one of the opposite side may stand within 10 yards (9.15 metres) of him.

Rule 11: A free kick may be taken in any manner the player chooses.

Rule 12: A goal is obtained when the ball goes out of the ground by passing between the posts had they been of sufficient height.

Rule 13: The ball when in play may be stopped by any part of the body, but may not be held or hit by the hands, arms, or shoulders.

Rule 14: All charging is fair; but holding, pushing with the hands, tripping up, and shinning are forbidden.

Where is Parker's Piece?

Parker's Piece is in the city of Cambridge, England. The 10-hectare (25-acre) park, which is a roughly square and completely flat plot of grass, has long been used as a playing pitch for soccer and cricket. In the 1800s it was owned by Trinity College and it was on the trees bordering this common that the Cambridge Rules of football were first posted.

Who was Richard Mulcaster?

Richard Mulcaster, who lived from 1531 to 1611, was headmaster of the Merchant Taylors' School and St. Paul's School in London. Not only was he a prominent educator of his time, he was also one of the greatest sixteenth-century advocates of soccer. In his 1581 publication titled "Positions Wherein Those Primitive Circumstances Be Examined, Which Are Necessarie for the Training up of Children," he argued that "Footeball" was beneficial "both to health and strength" of students, and he advocated for, organized, and refereed matches to counteract the craze of mob football.

> **Quickies**
> *Did you know ...*
> • Parker's Piece is named after Edward Parker, a cook, who held the original lease on the land and used it as a pasture?

Who was John Charles Thring?

In 1862, a the teacher at Uppingham School, in Rutland, England, named John Charles Thring, who was part of the group that had established the Cambridge Rules 1848, published an alternate set of soccer rules titled "The Simplest Game." Known as Uppingham Rules, they emphasized a non-violent approach to the game that was popular with other schools.

Who was Ebenezer Cobb Morley?

In 1863, Ebenezer Cobb Morley, the founder and captain of Barnes Football Club, wrote a letter to *Bell's Life* newspaper proposing a governing body for football. This letter resulted in a meeting of 12 soccer clubs taking place at the Freeman's Tavern in London in October 1863. England's Football Association was established at this meeting, with the aim of establishing a single unifying code for football. Ebenezer Cobb Morley was elected as the secretary of the Football Association and was later president.

When did soccer and rugby become separate sports?

When England's Football Association was established in 1863, they published the first set of rules, which expressly forbade carrying, passing, or otherwise handling the ball. Prior to this, the various codes of soccer used by clubs allowed players to use their hands to move the ball, often in a manner that resembled today's rugby. It is felt that the establishment of the first FA rules marked the break between soccer and rugby.

When did the FA Cup begin?

The 12 Founding Clubs of England's Football Association
- Barnes
- Blackheath
- Forest of Leytonstone
- Perceval House
- Kensington School
- The War Office
- Crystal Palace
- Epping Forest
- Crusaders
- Surbiton
- No Names of Kilburn
- Blackheath Proprietary School

In 1871, Charles W. Alcock, then FA secretary, announced the introduction of the Football Association Challenge Cup. It was the first knockout competition of its type in the world. Only 15 clubs took part in the first staging of the tournament. It included two clubs based in Scotland: Donington School and Queen's Park. In the 1872 final, the Wanderers beat the Royal Engineers 1–0 at the Kennington Oval. The FA Cup is the oldest association football competition in the world.

Who was the first professional soccer player on the international stage?

James Henry Forrest was an English soccer player whose career spanned the transition from amateur to professional in the 1880s and 1890s. He played most of his career for Blackburn Rovers, who were paying him £1 per week in 1885 when he was chosen to play for England in the Home Championship against Scotland, Ireland, and Wales. Despite complaints from Scottish officials that Forrest was a professional, he was allowed to play but he had to wear a different jersey from the rest of the team. Blackburn Rovers also had to agree not to pay him his wages in the week that he played for England.

> **Chronology of the Formation of the United Kingdom's Football Associations**
> - England: The Football Association (FA) — 1863
> - Scotland: The Scottish Football Association (SFA) — 1873
> - Wales: The Football Association of Wales (FAW) — 1876
> - Northern Ireland: Irish Football Association (IFA) — 1880

What England player was first to score against Scotland?

William Stanley-Kenyon of the Wanderers became England's first-ever goal scorer during their 4–2 win over Scotland on March 8, 1873. He scored two goals, and is therefore also the first player to score twice for England.

What was the Football Act of 1424?

The Football Act of 1424 was passed by the Parliament of Scotland during the reign of James I. It became law on May 26, 1424. The Act stated that "the king forbiddis that na man play at the fut ball under the payne of iiij d," which meant that playing football

> **Quickies**
> *Did you know ...*
> - England's longest unbeaten run stands at 20 matches played between a 3–2 loss to Scotland on April 13, 1889, and a 2–1 home defeat against Scotland on April 4, 1896? England's record during this seven-year period was 16 wins and 4 draws.

was made illegal, and punishable by a fine of four pence. The Act remained in force for several centuries, and was not repealed until the passing of the Statute Law Revision (Scotland) Act 1906. Obviously, it was one statute that did not take root.

When was the Scottish Football Association founded?

On March 13, 1873, representatives of seven Scottish soccer teams gathered at a meeting in Glasgow in response to an advertisement in the newspaper. The purpose of the gathering was to form the Scottish Football Association. At the meeting it was resolved that, "The clubs here represented form themselves into an association for the promotion of football according to the rules of The Football Association and that the clubs connected with this association subscribe for a challenge cup to be played for annually, the committee to propose the laws of the competition." An eighth club, Kilmarnock, did not attend the meeting, but expressed its wish to join by letter.

Founding clubs of the Scottish FA
• Queen's Park
• Clydesdale
• Vale of Leven
• Dumbreck
• Third Lanarkshire Rifle Volunteers
• Eastern
• Granville
• Kilmarnock

When was the Scottish Cup first played?

The Scottish Football Association Challenge Cup, usually known as the Scottish Cup, started in the 1873–74 season, when it was contested by 16 teams. The trophy is the oldest national trophy in the world. The Scottish Cup was first awarded to Queen's Park when they beat Clydesdale 2–0 in the final in front of a crowd of 3,000 people.

What is the Old Firm?

The Scottish soccer teams Celtic FC, founded in 1888, and Rangers FC, founded in 1873, both based in Glasgow, are collectively referred to as the Old Firm. It is not clear how this term came about. Some say it is because of camaraderie shown between the two clubs in their early days, while others surmise it is an ironic take on the arch rivalry that eventually developed between them. Whichever it is, the two clubs are indisputably the most successful in Scotland, having won between them 66 Scottish Cups and 93 Scottish Premier League championships as of 2008.

Quickies
Did you know ...
• the Scottish club Queen's Park FC, established in 1867, is the world's oldest soccer club outside of England?

Who was the Welsh Wizard?

Player Billy Meredith was born in Black Park, Wales, on July 28, 1874. He worked as a coal miner and played local soccer for Chirk, but at the age of 18 he signed as an amateur with Northwich Victoria, becoming the first Welshman to play for an English club. Two years later he joined Manchester City, but returned to Wales the following year to help his national team win their first international competition. He continued to work as a miner until 1896, when his club finally insisted he give up his colliery job. The fans loved Meredith's skills and dubbed him the "Welsh Wizard."

Teams in the Inaugural Scottish FA Cup Competition
• Queen's Park
• Clydesdale
• Alexandra Athletic
• Callander
• Granville
• Dumbarton
• Vale of Leven
• Eastern
• Rovers
• Dumbreck
• Renton
• Kilmarnock
• Third Lanarkshire Rifle Volunteers
• Southern
• Western
• Blythswood

What is the oldest Irish soccer club?

Cliftonville Football and Athletic Club, known as The Reds, is a Northern Irish football team playing in the IFA Premiership. Founded on September 20, 1879, in the north Belfast district of Cliftonville, they are the oldest football club in Ireland and celebrated their 125th anniversary in 2004.

Quickies

Did you know ...

• the Football Association of Wales, founded in 1876, is the third oldest national soccer association in the world?

Who was John McAlery?

While on his honeymoon to Scotland, Belfast businessman John McAlery attended a soccer match staged by the Scottish FA. McAlery so enjoyed the game that he returned home and placed an advertisement in the newspaper inviting players to join the "Cliftonville Association Football Club." At the time, there was no organized football association in Ireland. One week later, Cliftonville played its first match on September 20, 1879, losing 2–1 to a group of rugby players known as Quidnunces. In 1880, McAlery was the driving force behind the formation of the Irish FA, issuing an invitation to interested parties in Belfast and district to attend a meeting on November 18, 1880, at Queen's Hotel, from which the Irish Football Association was formed.

What 1882 game gave opposite records to Ireland and England?

On February 18, 1882, two years after the founding of the Irish FA, Ireland made their international debut against England, losing 13–0 in a friendly game played at Bloomfield Park in Belfast. This remains the record win for England and the record defeat for the Northern Ireland team.

When was the Irish league founded?

The Irish League is the second-oldest national league in the world, being formed a week earlier than the Scottish Football League. Only the Football League in England is older. Four clubs — Cliftonville, Glentoran, Linfield, and Lisburn Distillery — have retained membership of the Irish League since its inception in 1890.

> **Quickies**
> *Did you know ...*
> • Scotland's first match outside the British Isles was on May 26, 1929? They beat Norway 7–3 in Bergen.

When was the first international game between non-UK teams?

The first soccer international game played without involving a British side was between the United States and Canada, played in Newark, New Jersey, on November 28, 1885. The Canadians won 1–0.

> **Quickies**
> *Did you know ...*
> • Ireland changed to green shirts against England on October 17, 1931? Up until then they had worn blue.

What is the difference between the Irish Football Association (IFA) and the Football Association of Ireland (FAI)?

Ireland has two FAs because Ireland itself is divided into two nations, Northern Ireland, which is part of the United Kingdom, and the Republic of Ireland, which is a sovereign state formed in 1921. Beginning with the formation of the Irish Football Association (IFA) in 1879, all of Ireland was represented under that one association. But with the partition of Ireland in 1921, the Football Association of Ireland (FAI) was formed to represent the Republic of Ireland, due to bitter disputes between Dublin-area teams and Belfast teams.

> **Quickies**
> *Did you know ...*
> • it was not until 1952 that a team from outside Belfast was crowned champions of the Irish League, formed in 1890?

How did soccer become American football?

In 1884, the American Amateur Football Association was formed, the first such soccer organization outside Britain. Ten years later, the United States became the second country in the world to introduce professional soccer. However, in the 1870s, Harvard University opted for a rugby-style "handling game" over the "kicking game." As other universities followed Harvard's example, the handling game developed into the American form of football.

Quickies

Did you know ...

• England played their first game on foreign soil when they beat Austria 6–1 in Vienna on June 6, 1908?

What was the largest crowd to ever attend a soccer match?

The largest crowd ever to attend a soccer match was 199,854 spectators at the World Cup final in Rio de Janeiro, Brazil, on July 16, 1950. The game pitted Brazil against Uruguay. Uruguay won the match, 2–1.

Quickies

Did you know ...

• in 1930 the American national soccer team reached the semifinals of the inaugural soccer World Cup?

What were the longest shootouts in soccer history?

Two stand out. On November 20, 1988, during the 1988–89 Argentine Championship, Argentinos Juniors defeated Racing Club 20–19 on penalties after a 2–2 draw. The shootout required 44 kicks. Then on Jan 23, 2005, during the 2004–05 Tafel Lager Namibian FA Cup, KK Palace defeated Civics 17–16 on penalties after a 2–2 draw. The shootout required 48 kicks.

Quickies

Did you know ...

• the first professional soccer league in America was formed in 1894 but disbanded within months amid controversy over the importation of British players?

laws of the game

Who sets the official rules for soccer?

The official rules of soccer are called the Laws of the Game and they are maintained by two governing bodies: the International Football Association Board (IFAB) and the *Fédération Internationale de Football Association* (FIFA).

What is FIFA?

FIFA is an acronym for *Fédération Internationale de Football Association*. It is the international governing body of association football, headquartered in Zurich, Switzerland. FIFA is responsible for the organization and governance of soccer's major international tournaments, most notably the FIFA World Cup, held since 1930. The Laws of the Game are not solely the responsibility of FIFA; they are maintained by a body called the International Football Association Board (IFAB). FIFA has members on its board (four representatives); the other four are provided by the football associations of the United Kingdom: England, Scotland, Wales, and Northern Ireland, in recognition of their contribution to the creation and history of the game. Changes to the Laws of the Game must be agreed upon by at least six of the eight delegates.

The Eight FIFA Presidents Since Its Founding in 1904

- Robert Guerin, France — 1904–06
- Daniel Burley Woolfall, England — 1906–18
- Jules Rimet, France — 1921–54
- Rodolphe William Seeldrayers, Belgium — 1954–55
- Arthur Drewry, England — 1955–61
- Sir Stanley Rous, England — 1961–74
- João Havelange, Brazil — 1974–98
- Joseph S. Blatter, Switzerland — 1998–present

What is IFAB?

IFAB is an acronym for the International Football Association Board. Established in England in 1886, the board was originally made up of the United Kingdom's four pioneering football associations: England's Football Association (The FA), the Scottish Football Association (SFA), the Football Association of Wales (FAW),

and Northern Ireland's Irish Football Association (IFA). Its aim was to create a
unified set of rules for the game in Great
Britain and function as a governing body.
Each of the four founding FAs had equal

voting rights on the board. Beginning in 1913, the *Fédération Interna-*
tionale de Football Association (FIFA), which governs world association
soccer, became a voting board member. Today, each UK association has
one vote on the board and FIFA has four. IFAB deliberations must be
approved by at least six votes. Thus, FIFA's approval is necessary for any
IFAB decision, but FIFA alone cannot change the Laws of the Game; they
need to be agreed by at least two of the UK members.

How many referees are there in a regulation soccer match?

There are three. One referee (sometimes called the centre referee),
and two assistant referees (formerly called linesmen) who patrol the
perimeter of the field and carry flags to signal to the referee. The referee,
who is the only one of the three who conducts his duties in bounds on
the pitch, is the ruling authority for any given soccer match. His word is
law on the pitch.

What is the technical area?

The technical area is a marked-off zone at pitch-side where a team
manager, other coaching personnel, and player substitutes are required
to confine themselves during matches. According to the Laws of the
Game, the technical area is marked by a white line, "1 metre (1 yard)
on either side of the designated seated area and extend[ing] forward up
to a distance of 1 metre (1 yard) from the touch line." Substitutes are
allowed to leave the technical area to warm up prior to entering a match.
Managers and coaching staff may not cross the line during play, except

in special cases, such as medical personnel attending to an injured player. The technical area falls under the supervision of the fourth official.

What is the fourth official?

The fourth official is essentially a support person to the referee who can, when needed, step in as a backup assistant referee when one of the designated assistants cannot perform his duties. The fourth official assists with administrative duties surrounding the match. Stationed pitch-side, he is responsible for assisting with substitution procedures during the match. He has the authority to check the equipment of substitutes before they enter the field of play. He supervises the replacement of game balls. He must indicate to the referee when the wrong player is cautioned because of mistaken identity or when a player is not sent off after having been shown two yellow cards or when violent conduct occurs out of the view of the referee and assistant referees. After the match, the fourth official must submit a report to the appropriate authorities on any misconduct or other incident that occurred out of the view of the referee and the assistant referees. He also has the authority to inform the referee of irresponsible behaviour by anyone in the technical area.

The Five Duties of the Assistant Referees (subject to the decision of the referee)
- Indicate when the whole of the ball has passed out of the field of play.
- Indicate which side is entitled to a corner kick, goal kick or throw-in.
- Indicate when a player may be penalized for being in an offside position.
- Indicate when a substitution is requested.
- Indicate when misconduct or any other incident has occurred out of the view of the referee.

Who was Ken Aston?

The red and yellow card system was invented by English referee Ken Aston, whose innovation was inspired one day in the late 1960s by the yellow "caution" and red "stop" lights in the streets of London. Aston sat on FIFA's

Referee's Committee from 1970 to 1972. His card system was first used at the 1970 World Cup. Aston died on October 23, 2001 at the age of 86.

What does a yellow card mean?

The yellow card is a caution issued to a player by the referee. The yellow card may be shown to a player who is guilty of unsporting behaviour, shows dissent by word or action, persistently infringes the Laws of the Game, delays the restart of play, fails to respect the required distance when play is restarted with a corner kick or a free kick, enters or re-enters the field of play without the referee's permission, or deliberately leaves the field of play without the referee's permission. Any time a yellow or red card is shown, a "direct" or "indirect kick" will also be awarded.

What does a red card mean?

When a player is shown a red card it means ejection from the game. By the Laws of the Game, a player must be shown a red card for serious foul play, violent conduct, spitting at an opponent or any other person, deliberately handling the ball in an attempt to prevent an obvious scoring opportunity, denying an obvious goal-scoring opportunity to an opponent moving toward the player's goal by an offence punishable by a free kick or a penalty kick, and for using offensive, insulting, or abusive language. A player will also be shown a red card and ejected immediately after receiving a second yellow card caution in the same match.

What's the difference between yellow and red card offenses?

Yellow card offenses generally cover acts that demonstrate poor sportsmanship and disrupt the game, but don't directly affect the score or cause injury. For example, a player might receive a yellow card for a succession of "ordinary" fouls, despite a warning from the referee. This is called "persistent infringement." Players will also be shown a yellow card for "unsporting behaviour," which covers almost any action that shows disregard for fair play but is not extremely violent. Red card offenses are much more serious acts that go completely against the spirit of the game (called "serious foul play" in game parlance). This is behaviour that should never occur on a soccer field regardless of how a game is going.

What does it mean when the referee holds his arms straight out?

This is called "advantage" and it means that the referee has seen a foul but has decided not to call it yet because the fouled team is in an advantageous position and might possibly score. Advantage generally only lasts three to five seconds before the referee will blow his whistle and stop play.

What does it mean when the referee blows his whistle and points at a goal?

The referee has seen a foul and is awarding a direct free kick against the goal he is pointing to.

Why does the referee sometime hold his arm straight up in the air during a free kick?

When a free kick is awarded, according to the Laws of the Game the only signal a referee is required to give to distinguish a direct free kick from an indirect free kick is to raise his arm straight in the air. The raised arm signals that an indirect free kick has been awarded. On a direct free kick the kicker may score

from the kick, but on an indirect free kick, the ball must touch a second player (on either team, including the goalkeeper) before going into the goal in order for the score to count. The referee will only lower his arm when the ball has touched that second player (or gone out of bounds). On an indirect free kick, the kicker may not touch the ball again until the referee's arm comes down.

How do players know when a penalty kick is awarded?

When a referee points directly at the 18-yard (16.5-metre) area, he is awarding a penalty kick. The referee will usually run to the penalty spot, stop beside it, and point straight down at it with his hand.

Assistant Referee Flag Signals Decoded

• Flag straight up: indicating to the referee to stop play because assistant referee needs to talk to referee. Can also mean offside or be a signal for the referee to look at the other linesman.
• Flag straight up with hand held over his chest badge: indicating to referee that a player needs to be shown a yellow or red card.
• Flag out sideways at 45 degrees horizontally along the touchline: indicating for a throw-in. The team attacking in the direction they are pointing takes the throw.
• Flag pointing at the goal: indicating a goal kick.
• Flag pointed at the corner flag: indicating a corner kick.
• Flag held straight out in front of assistant referee after an offside call:
    - Up at a 45-degree angle: indicating an offside on the far side of the field.
    - Straight horizontally: indicating an offside in the middle of the field.
    - Down at a 45-degree angle: indicating an offside on the near side of the field.
• Flag held straight up suspended between both hands: substitution in progress.
• Flag held horizontally across chest: calling for penalty kick.
• Flag held behind back while standing at corner flag: calling for penalty kick.
• Flag held up after a goal: assistant referee wishes to dispute the goal.

What is the ruling when a ball bursts after a kick but still goes into the net?

Even if the ball is headed into the net for a goal, if it bursts or deflates at any point while in play, the Laws of the Game require that play must be stopped and restarted with the new ball at the point where the ball first became defective, which means a goal cannot be scored with a burst ball. If the ball deflates *after* crossing the goal line, it is a goal.

Can coaches or players change the game ball?

No. If a coach or player feels the game ball is defective, they must bring their concerns to the attention of the referee or one of the game officials (who will then tell the referee). The only person on the field who may change the game ball is the referee. Any attempt on the part of a coach or player, or anyone else, to change the game ball, can be ruled as misconduct and lead to ejection.

Quickies

Did you know ...

• a substitute who has not properly completed the substitution procedure by setting foot onto the field of play cannot restart play by taking a throw-in or corner kick?

What should a coach do upon realizing his team has fielded too many players?

The coach should learn to count better, because someone on his team is about to get a yellow card and possibly worse if the situation is handled poorly. Since it is illegal for a player to leave the pitch without the permission of the referee, the coach should tell the player who is coming off to stand on the field just inside the touchline at the half-line. The coach should then get the assistant referee's attention and explain the problem. The assistant referee will notify the referee that his player is coming off, whereupon the referee will yellow-card his player as required by the Laws of the Game. If the coach simply tells a player to come off the field, that player will receive two yellow cards — one for being the extra player, one for leaving the pitch without permission — and then, of course, they will also receive an automatic red card, which means ejection from the game.

Can a goalkeeper switch places during a game with another player?

Yes, this is permitted under the Laws of the Game, provided that the referee is informed before the change is made (otherwise, both players will be shown the yellow card), and that the change is made only during a stoppage in play. Since it is also required under the Laws of the Game that the goalkeeper wear a different-coloured jersey, both players will also have to change jerseys.

Who was Horst Eckel?

Striker Horst Eckel found his place in the annals of soccer by becoming the first-ever substitute player. Up until the 1954 FIFA World Cup, substitutions were illegal in soccer. If one of the 11 players who started the game for a team was injured and had to leave the pitch, the team had to play out the match one short — or two, or three, or however many players eventually left the pitch. And at no point could a player from the bench come on to relieve another player. On October 11, 1953, during a qualifying match against Saarland for the 1954 World Cup, Horst Eckel, who played for West Germany, became the first-ever substitute under new rules instituted by FIFA for the tournament.

Five Laws of the Game that Specifically Concern the Goalkeeper

The goalkeeper may not:

1. take more than four steps while controlling the ball with his hands before releasing it from his possession;
2. touch the ball again with his hands after it has been released from his possession and has not touched any other player;
3. touch the ball with his hands after it has been deliberately kicked to him by a teammate;
4. touch the ball with his hands after he has received it directly from a throw-in taken by a teammate;
5. waste time.

When are socks illegal?

As everyone knows, the referee is God and King on the soccer pitch, having the first and final word regarding all interpretations of the Laws of the Game. The question of what is "unsporting conduct" is intentionally left open to interpretation, so that the referee can deal with unusual cases and incidents. For example, if a player wears a different-coloured pair of socks than the rest of his team, it suddenly becomes easier for someone in possession of the ball dribbling up the field, head down and concentrating, to spot that player. A bright red pair of socks on a striker, for instance, will stand out against the green turf. There is no strict provision against this tactic in the Laws of the Game, but players shouldn't expect to get away with it. The referee has power even over players' uniforms, and a good one will not allow mismatched socks, and might even call this unsporting behaviour and give that striker yellow card for trying — both literally and figuratively — to pull a fast one with his red socks.

The Laws of the Game Governing Substitutions

To replace a player with a substitute, the following conditions must be observed: ·

- the referee must be informed before any proposed substitution is made;
- the substitute only enters the field of play after the player being replaced has left and after receiving a signal from the referee;
- the substitute only enters the field of play at the halfway line and during a stoppage in the match;
- the substitution is completed when a substitute enters the field of play;
- from that moment, the substitute becomes a player and the player he has replaced becomes a substituted player;
- the substituted player takes no further part in the match;
- all substitutes are subject to the authority and jurisdiction of the referee, whether called upon to play or not.

What is a "club" linesman?

A "club" linesman is simply one who is not a certified referee, usually recruited shortly before the match from among the more knowledgeable soccer spectators on hand to serve when a certified linesman is

Quickies

Did you know ...

- there is no stipulation in the Laws of the Game that require numbers on jerseys?

not available. Under the Laws of the Game "club" linesmen are limited with respect to the matters they may call to assist the referee.

Why do games that are not tied at the end of regulation time often go longer?

One of the unique things about soccer is that during a match no one on or off the pitch knows exactly how long the match will go. That's because the referee is the official timekeeper, and while regulations state that a match consists of two halves of 45 minutes each, with a mandatory break at halftime, they also state that the referee has discretion to add time to the end of each half for any stoppage of play. While the rules for games like hockey, basketball, and American football include provisions for stopping the clock (such as after a goal, or for out of bounds), the clock for a soccer game never stops, except for the during the halftime break. The referee is under no obligation to tell anyone how much additional time will be added to each half. The clock runs out only when the referee says so.

Quickies
Did you know ...
- a "club" linesman can call the ball in or out over the touchline or goal lines, and can signal to the referee which team is entitled to possession of balls gone out of play, but they cannot signal for offside, or for fouls committed outside the sight of the referee.

Why do some referees actually stop the clock?

Strictly speaking, such referees are in violation of the Laws of the Game. This generally only happens at the amateur level. The referee has a stopwatch and, as the official timekeeper for the match, is supposed to add extra time to the end of each half for any stoppage of play. If, for example, a player is injured and it takes two minutes to get that player off the field and

Quickies
Did you know ...
- aside from during the regulation halftime beak, the Laws of the Game do not permit the referee to ever stop the clock once play has begun?

resume play, the referee should add two minutes to the end of the half. The referee is supposed to keep track of such stoppages in a notebook, but the simpler method is to stop the stopwatch for two minutes, thus suspending the game clock and negating the need to keep track of how long the stoppage is. The main problem with this lazy and illegal method of timekeeping is that the ref can sometimes forget to re-start the stopwatch. Also, if the clock is stopped too often or for insignificant reasons, the ref may be stuck with the dilemma of whether to call the game a bit "early" by the official watch.

What if time expires before a penalty shot can be taken?

If a foul requiring a penalty shot is called before time in a half or game expires, but the clock expires before the penalty shot can be taken, the penalty shot must be taken before the half or game can officially end. In such instances, the penalty-taker gets only one touch of the ball, so they had better make it a good kick, because whether they score a goal or not, the play ends the moment ball goes out of bounds or its momentum is spent.

What is the correct procedure for a kickoff?

In a kickoff, each team must be in their respective defending half of the field and the team opposing the kickoff may not have any players within 10 yards (9.15 metres) of the ball. The ball is in play the moment it is kicked and moves forward at all; even stepping on it and causing it to bobble forward slightly is enough.

What's the ruling if a ball hits the referee and rebounds into the goal?

The referee, like the corner flag, or a goal post, or the ground itself, is merely part of the field of play. If the ball hits the referee, play should continue just as if the ball bounced off a rock. And if the ball bounces off the ref into the goal, it is a goal!

The Seven Ways a Ball Can Be Put into Play

* kickoff
* throw-in
* goal kick
* corner kick
* free kick
* penalty kick
* drop ball

What is a "speaking captain"?

Unlike other sports, a soccer team can have more than one captain. This allowance holds over from days when substitutions were illegal and it was advisable to have more than one captain in case any one of them got injured or sent off. During a coin-toss meeting before the start of a match, when the captains and the referee are assembled near the centre of the field, if either team sent more than one captain, the referee will ask which one is the "speaking captain," meaning which one is authorized to make binding decisions at the meeting.

Quickies
Did you know ...
* a ball rolling along outside the touchline remains in play as long as part of the ball is over the touchline?

What happens at a coin-toss meeting?

Exact procedures can vary from place to place and from referee to referee, but the basics are as follows: When all the teams' captains and the referee gather near the centre of the field, the referee makes note of the numbers (and maybe the names)

Quickies
Did you know ...
* on a free kick, the ball must move forward on the initial contact? Even the tiniest fraction will suffice, before a rearward pass can be made. Prior to 1997, the ball had to move its full circumference on the ground in a free kick.

of the teams' speaking captains. Then one team's speaking captain will be chosen at the referee's discretion to call the coin toss. After the toss, the referee will ask the winner which end they want to defend, and then make sure everyone present is clear on which end they will attack and which they will defend at the start the game. The referee then tells the losing side that they will kick off, and the meeting is over.

Why does the referee point at the centre of the field and not the goal to indicate a goal?

The regulation restart method after either team scores a goal is a kickoff by the other team from the centre of the field. That is why the referee points at the centre of the field after a goal. The referee is not indicating a goal, but rather calling for a restart from the centre of the field.

What is the penalty for faking an injury?

Not that this ever, ever happens (ahem!), but any simulating action that is intended to deceive the referee — anywhere on the field — must be sanctioned as unsporting behaviour. This includes Oscar-worthy performances for fake injuries. The penalty is not a golden statue, but a yellow card.

Regulation Method for a Throw-in

1. The player doing the throw-in faces the field of play.
2. The player has part of each foot either on the touchline or on the ground outside the touchline.
3. The player uses both hands to throw the ball.
4. The player delivers the ball from behind and over his head.

What is the penalty for showboating?

There is little in sports that is more annoying than watching an athlete — especially one from the opposing team —

ungracefully celebrate a goal with showboating. FIFA agrees, because rules state, "While it is permissible for a player to demonstrate his joy when a goal has been scored, the celebration must not be excessive." In the Laws of the Game, referees are specifically instructed to issue a caution when a goal-scorer makes gestures which are provocative, derisory, or inflammatory, climbs on a perimeter fence, removes his shirt over his head, or covers his head with his shirt.

What is the difference between "impeding" and "obstruction"?

If a player is not playing the ball, but is preventing someone else from moving toward the ball, he is impeding the other player. That is a foul. This used to be called "obstruction," and often still is, but FIFA prefers that the term "obstruction" be reserved for when a player in possession of the ball blocks another player from getting to the ball, which, when performed in the right manner, is not a foul, but a matter of skill.

When is a player offside?

Provided that he is not in his own half of the field, a player is offside when he is not in possession of the ball and he is nearer to his opponents' goal line than both the ball and the second last opponent (including the goalkeeper). If an offside infraction is called, the opponent is awarded an indirect free kick (IFK). There is no offside offence if a player receives the ball directly from a goal kick, a throw-in, or a corner kick.

Regulation Procedure For a Kickoff

- All players must be in their own half of the field.
- The opponents of the team taking the kickoff must be at least 10 yards (9.15 metres) from the ball until it is in play.
- The ball is stationary on the centre mark.
- The referee gives a signal.
- The ball is in play when it is kicked and moves forward any amount.
- The kicker may not touch the ball again until it has touched another player.

Should a player always be penalized for being offside?

No. As with so much else on the soccer pitch, it is up to the discretion of the referee whether or not to call a player offside. A player in an offside position is usually only penalized if, at the moment the ball touches or is played by one of his team, he is, in the opinion of the referee, involved in active play by interfering with play, interfering with an opponent, or gaining an advantage by being in that position.

When is offside position determined?

Offside position is not determined at the time the ball is received by an attacker, but rather it is determined at the moment the ball was last played by one of the attacker's teammates. If, for example, an attacker kicks the ball high in the air toward the opponent's goal while none of his teammates are in offside position, but then a second speedy attacker penetrates the defence and receives the kick behind the second-last opponent, the speedy one is not offside.

What should the ruling be if the ball simply ricochets off an attacker in an offside position?

It is not actually necessary to *play* the ball to be called for an offside infraction. A player in an offside position could be tying his shoelaces and not even watching the play, but if the ball ricochets off him, and, in the eyes of the referee, his team gains advantage from his position, the attacking team should be called for offside.

What happens when a player with a penalty kick, kicks the ball before the referee signals that it is okay to do so?

Only the referee can tell a penalty kicker when it is okay to take the kick. If the kicker takes the kick before that signal and the ball enters the goal, the kick will have to be retaken. If the ball does not enter the goal, the kick is not retaken, and the kicker has lost a chance to score.

What happens when, during a penalty kick, the defending goalkeeper moves off the goal line before the ball has been kicked?

According to the Laws of the Game, during a penalty kick the defending goalkeeper may not move off the goal line until the ball has been kicked and is in forward motion. If the goalkeeper does move off the goal line in such a situation, the referee should allow the kick to proceed. If the ball enters the goal, a goal is awarded, but if the ball does not enter the goal, the kick should be retaken.

Fouls That Will Lead to a Direct Free Kick*

- Kicking or attempting to kick an opponent.
- Tripping or attempting to trip an opponent.
- Jumping at an opponent in a careless or reckless manner, or with excessive force.
- Charging an opponent in a careless or reckless manner, or with excessive force.
- Striking or attempting to strike an opponent.
- Pushing an opponent.
- Making contact with the opponent before the ball when tackling.
- Holding an opponent.
- Spitting at an opponent.
- Handling the ball deliberately (except for the goalkeeper within his own penalty area).

* If any of these are committed by a player inside his own penalty area, a penalty kick is awarded.

Who was William McCrumb?

At the June 1890 general meeting of the International Football Association Board, the Irish FA submitted a proposal to introduce a new rule to stop the practice of defenders fouling an attacking player in order to prevent a goal. It was the penalty kick, and the idea came

Fouls That Will Lead to an Indirect Free Kick

By a goalkeeper inside his own penalty area:

- holding the ball in hands for longer than six seconds;
- handling the ball after it has been released from his possession but has not yet touched another player;
- handling the ball after it has been deliberately kicked to him by a teammate;
- handling the ball after he has received it directly from a throw-in taken by a teammate.

By any player:

- playing in a dangerous manner;
- impeding the progress of an opponent;
- preventing the goalkeeper from releasing the ball from his hands; or
- at the discretion of the referee, offences not covered under the Fouls and Conduct section (Law 12) of the Laws of the Game, for which play is stopped to caution or dismiss a player.

Quickies

Did you know ...

- the defenders do not have a right to sufficient time to set up their defense along the goal line for indirect free kicks awarded inside the defender's goal area? The attackers can take an immediate restart if it is to their advantage — regardless of the where the defending players are standing.

from prominent Irish businessman William McCrumb, who had himself played goal for Milford Everton FC in the first season of the Irish Football League. McCrumb's original proposal read: "If any player shall intentionally trip or hold an opposing player, or deliberately handle the ball within 12 yards (11 metres) from his own goal line, the referee shall, on appeal, award the opposing side a penalty kick, to be taken from any point 12 yards (11 metres) from the goal line, under the following conditions: All players, with the exception of the player taking the penalty kick and the goalkeeper, shall stand behind the ball and at least six yards (5.5 metres) from it; the ball shall be in play when the kick is taken. A goal may be scored from a penalty kick." After much discussion and deliberation, the penalty kick was introduced in the 1891–92 season. The first-ever penalty kick was awarded to the Wolverhampton Wanderers in a game against Accrington Stanley at Molineux on September 14, 1891. The penalty was taken and scored by John Heath and Wolverhampton went on to win the game 5–0.

What is the difference between a "handball" and "handling" a ball?

A "handball" is when the ball strikes a player (other than the goalkeeper) on the hand or arm and there is no intent on the part of the player struck to control the ball with either hand or arm. As such, a "handball" is not illegal. If the player attempts in any way to control the ball with hand or arm it is called "handling" the ball, and is an illegal play.

Quickies
Did you know ...
• soccer goalkeepers didn't have to wear different-coloured shirts prior to 1913?

on the pitch

Why is the field for soccer called a "pitch"?

This is a holdover from the earliest days of organized soccer in Great Britain when, not having a designated soccer field on which to play, school teams such as Eton and Cambridge would play on the local cricket pitch. This of course, begs the question, why is the field for cricket called a "pitch"? That is because in the early days of cricket, when the wickets were stuck into the ground the action was called "pitching the wickets." The word "pitch" in this instance means to thrust or drive a stake into the ground, just as with pitching a tent. Its origin is unknown.

Quickies
Did you know ...
- the Laws of the Game do not require the playing pitch to be made of natural grass — but they do require it to be green?

When were the first field markings used?

The first field markings in soccer appeared in 1891, when new rules required that goal lines and touch lines be marked, as well as a centre circle, the goalkeepers' areas, and a 12-yard (11-metre) line from the goal. A penalty kick could be taken from anywhere along that 12-yard line. An optional 18-yard (16.5-metre) line across the full width of the pitch was also introduced to denote the penalty area. Modern pitch markings came into being in 1902, with an added halfway line, goal areas, penalty areas, and the penalty spots.

Quickies
Did you know ...
- the penalty arc is the only part of the football pitch markings that did not originate in Britain? It was added in 1937 at the recommendation of various European football associations.

What are "touchlines"?

Quite simply, the touchlines on a soccer pitch are the playing area's sidelines. One of the most unusual aspects of the game is that a player in possession of the ball may physically cross outside the touchline without being out of bounds, so long as a portion of the ball is still inside or over the touchline. The *whole* ball must cross the line to be out of bounds. The same is true along the goal lines, or "end lines," which mark the boundaries for the ends of the playing field.

When were the first goalposts used in soccer?

That would be way back in 1681 when a match was played between servants of the King, and those of the Duke of Albemarle. The doorways of two forts were used as goals, and players attempted to score by driving the ball through one of the doorways.

Regulation Soccer Pitch Dimensions

Domestic Matches
Length (touchline):
minimum 100 yards (90 metres)
maximum 130 yards (120 metres);
Width (goal line): minimum 45 yards (45 metres) maximum 100 yards (90 metres).

International Matches
Length (touchline):
minimum 110 yards (100 metres)
maximum 120 yards (110 metres);
Width (goal line): minimum 70 yards (64 metres) maximum 80 yards (75 metres).

When was the size of the goal determined?

In 1863 the English Football Association decreed that the goal posts should be 8 yards (7.32 metres) apart. In 1866, they further decreed that posts should be 8 feet (2.44 metres) high. Both measurements stand today.

Have goal posts always been elliptical in shape?

No. The elliptical goal posts of today's professional game were introduced in 1920 by J.C. Perkins of the Standard Goals Company in Nottingham, England. Prior to that, goalposts were either round or square, but the elliptical shape took over because it

is much stronger. Nottingham Forest was
the first club in the world to try them.

When were the first goal nets used?

In 1891, Liverpool engineer John Alexander Brodie decided to design "a huge pocket" for the back of the goal to stop not only the ball from escaping, but also to halt disputes about whether a goal had been scored or not. As a result, the world's first footballer to ever "put the ball in the back of the net" was Fred Geary of Everton, at a trial game in Nottingham, England, on New Year's Day that same year. The first FA Cup final to use nets was played at the Kennington Oval in 1892 with West Bromwich Albion beating Aston Villa 3–0.

What happens if the crossbar of the goal becomes dislodged or damaged during a match?

FIFA, the world governing body of soccer, makes special mention of this in the Laws of the Game. "If the crossbar becomes displaced or broken, play is stopped until it has been repaired or replaced in position. If a repair is not possible, the match is abandoned. The use of a rope to replace the crossbar is not permitted. If the crossbar is repaired, the match is restarted with a dropped ball at the place where the ball was located when the play was stopped."

What is the purpose of the penalty arc?

Often called "the D," the penalty arc at the top of the penalty area in front of the goal is there to make sure all players (except for the penalty-taker,

The Positions of Play on the Pirch

• Goalkeeper (GK)
• Defenders
  - Centre-back (CB)
  - Sweeper/Libero (SW)
  - Fullback (FB/RB/LB)
  - Wingback (WB/RWB/LWB)
• Midfielders
  - Centre midfielder (CM)
  - Defensive midfielder (DM)
  - Attacking midfielder (AM)
  - Winger (RW/LW) or wide midfielder (LM/RM)
• Forward
  - Centre forward (CF)
  - Striker (S)
  - Deep-lying forward (SS)

of course) are 10 yards (9.14 metres) away from the ball when a penalty kick is taken. Only the penalty-taker can stand within this arc during the kick. The arc is necessary because the top of the penalty area can be sometimes be as close as six yards from the penalty spot.

How many players are allowed to play for a team in a soccer match?

Soccer teams may consist of a maximum of 11 on-field players (and a minimum of seven) with three substitutes allowed per game. If, due to injuries or other reasons, a team cannot field seven players, the match is cancelled.

What is a "utility player"?

In soccer, like other sports, a utility player is one who can play many positions. This will commonly be defense and midfield, sometimes defense and attack, a few outfield players have also made competent substitute goalkeepers.

What is a striker?

A striker is a scoring forward, usually a centre forward who is highly skilled at putting the ball in the net. The striker often plays "pushed up" into a offensive position leading the formation, while much of the rest of the team works the wings, feeding the striker or defence. Many great strikers have poor defensive skills, and are called "pure strikers." The striker traditionally wears the number 10 jersey.

What is a "sweeper"?

"Sweeper" is the name for a versatile fullback player who "sweeps up" the ball if the opponent manages to breach the defensive line. Unlike other defenders, the sweeper does not mark, or cover, one particular opponent, but covers the centre of defense. The *verrou* system in Switzerland and the *catenaccio* system in Italy were both notable for employing sweepers.

What does it mean when I see a team's formation described in numbers, such as 2-3-5 or 4-4-2?

This is a method of indicating the number of outfielders in each zone of the formation. It does not include the goalkeeper, but counts forward from the defensive line, so 2-3-5, for

Nine Notable Utility Players
- Michael Essien, Chelsea: midfield, defence
- Juliano Belletti, Chelsea: midfield, defence
- Phil Neville, Everton: midfield, defence
- John O'Shea, Manchester United: defence, midfield, occasionally goalkeeper
- Phil Jagielka, Everton: defence, midfield, substitute goalkeeper
- Chris Sutton, retired: striker, defender, midfielder
- Paul Madeley, retired: every position except goalkeeper
- Sandy Brown, retired: every position including goalkeeper
- Martin Peters, retired: every position including goalkeeper

Sixteen Sensational Strikers
- Dimitar Berbatov, Bulgaria, Manchester United
- Omar Bravo, Mexico, Deportivo La Coruña
- Didier Drogba, Ivory Coast, Chelsea
- Thierry Henry, France, FC Barcelona
- Miroslav Klose, Gemany, Bayer München
- Henrik Larsson, Sweden, Helsingborgs
- Lionel Messi, Argentina, FC Barcelona
- Lukas Podolski, Gemany, Bayer München
- Robinho, Brazil, Manchester City
- Ronaldo, Brazil, Corinthians
- Wayne Rooney, England, Manchester United
- Hakan Şükür, Turkey, Galatasaray
- Luca Toni, Italy, Bayer München
- Fernando Torres, Spain, Liverpool
- David Trézéguet, France, Juventus
- Ruud van Nistelrooy, Netherlands, Real Madrid

Seventeen Super Soccer Sweepers
• Alexandru Apolzan: Romanian, CCA Bucharest
• Roberto Ayala: Argentine, Real Zaragoza (Spain)
• Karim Bagheri: Iranian, Persepolis FC
• Franco Baresi: Italian, AC Milan
• Franz Beckenbauer: German, FC Bayern Munich
• Miodrag Belodedici: Romanian, Steaua Bucharest and Red Star Belgrade
• Horst Blankenburg: German, Ajax Amsterdam and Hamburger SV
• Emad El-Nahhas: Egyptian, Al-Ahly (Cairo)
• Daniel Passarella: Argentine, River Plate (Buenos Aires)
• Armando Picchi: Italian, FC Internazionale Milano
• Ronald Koeman: Dutch, Ajax Amsterdam, PSV Eindhoven
• Mo Konjić: Bosnian, FK Sloboda Tuzla, NK Belišće, NK Zagreb
• Matthias Sammer: German, Dynamo Dresden
• Lothar Matthäus: German, Bayern Munich
• Hans-Uwe Pilz: German, Dynamo Dresden
• Gaetano Scirea: Italian, Juventus (Turin)
• Tonono: Spainish, UD Las Palmas (Canary Islands)

example, would consist of one row of two defenders, one row of three midfielders, and one row of five forwards.

What does *verrou* mean?

The *verrou* or "chain" is a system of play invented by Karl Rappan while coach of Switzerland in the 1930s and 1940s. It was the first system to use four players on defence, employing a sweeper called the *verrouilleur* — a highly defensive fullback who patrolled the centre of defense ahead of the goalkeeper. The *verrou* system also required players to switch positions and duties depending on the game's pattern. It was used by the Swiss national tem in the 1938 World Cup to knock out Nazi Germany in the first round. The *catenaccio* system of Italy evolved out of the *verrou* system.

What does *catenaccio* mean?

Catenaccio is Italian for "bolt," as in a door bolt, and in soccer it refers to a tactical formation made famous in Italy during the 1960s by coach Helenio Herrera and FC *Internazionale Milano* (Inter Milan). It uses a strong defensive formation, such as 1-3-3-3 or 1-4-4-1, which implements a fullback called a "sweeper," who stands in front of the goalkeeper and patrols the centre of defense. From the 1970s to the 1990s, *catenaccio* became a trademark playing style of the Italian national team. The system, often criticized for its lack of offensive creativity, was nonetheless effective, employing sudden strikes to score early in a game and then relying on defence to protect the lead.

What is the WM system?

The WM system was created in the mid-1920s by manager Herbert Chapman (of Arsenal) to counter a change in the offside law in 1925. The change had reduced the number of opposition players that attackers needed between themselves and the goal line from three to two. This led to the introduction of a centre-back to stop the opposing centre-forward, and tried to balance defensive and offensive playing. The WM system employs three backs, four midfielders, and three forwards, and is so called because in a formation diagram the groupings look like an M under a W, with one player at each point of each letter.

What is Total Football?

Total Football is the term used to describe an influential theory of tactical soccer in which any of a team's players on the field can take over the role of any teammate. The foundations for Total Football were laid by Jack Reynolds, who was the manager of Ajax Amsterdam from 1915–1925, 1928–1940, and 1945–1947. Rinus Michels, who played under Reynolds, later went on to become manager of Ajax himself and refined the concept into what is known today as "Total Football" (*Totaalvoetbal* in Dutch). In Total Football, a player who moves out of his position is replaced by another from his team, thus retaining the team's intended organizational structure. In this fluid system, no player is fixed in his nominal role; anyone can be successively an attacker, a midfielder, and a defender.

What is Gaelic football?

Gaelic football is an Irish offshoot of the violent medieval game *mêlée*. In the modern game, sides are limited to 15 players. Players may not throw the ball, but may dribble it with hand or foot and may punch or punt it toward their opponents' goal. Goals count as either one or three points, depending on whether the ball passes above (one) or below (three) a crossbar attached to the goalposts.

Who wore the first shin guards?

Shin guards, which are now required kit under the Laws of the Game, were first introduced in 1874 by Sam Widdowson, a player for Nottingham Forest. Widdowson cut down a pair of cricket shin pads and strapped them to the outside of his stockings. He was initially ridiculed, but the protective value of the pads could not be denied and they eventually caught on.

What are molded studs?

The most common type of soccer shoe are molded stud shoes, which are very versatile and can be used on dry grass, wet grass, and light mud. They have 12 to 16 molded plastic or rubber studs in the soles that look like black gum drops. The large number of studs gives better support over a wide area.

What are six-stud cleats?

When the ground is very muddy and soft, soccer shoes called six-stud cleats are often used. These shoes have six screw-in studs in the sole. One advantage of six-stud cleats is that in such conditions the mud does not pack up between the studs. Another is that cleats can be changed to shorter or longer depending on the ground conditions. An extra set of studs is cheaper than a second pair of shoes.

What are blades?

These sound more sinister than they are. A soccer shoe with "blades" uses a series of elliptical tooth-like studs around the periphery of the sole. A more recent innovation, these boots are said to make turning easier.

What is the "Acme Thunderer"?

Through the 1860s and 1870s, Joseph Hudson, an English toolmaker from Birmingham, was using his home bathroom as a whistle-making workshop, but it wasn't until 1884 that he invented the Acme Thunderer, which is credited as the world's first reliable pea whistle and quickly became the whistle of choice for British soccer referees.

Some Whistles Models Used on Soccer Pitches

• 1884 Acme Thunderer
• 1920 Acme Thunderer, model 60.5
• 1930 Pro-Soccer whistle
• 1988 Tornado 2000
• 1989 Acme Tornado
• 2004 Tornado, models 622 and 635, and the Thunderer 560
• 2004 Fox 40 pealess whistle

How can you tell if a ball is regulation-approved?

There are three markings to look for in order to prove that a ball has been tested to comply with International Football Association regulations: (1) the official "FIFA APPROVED" logo, (2) the official "FIFA Inspected" logo, and (3)

Specifications For Soccer Ball
An International Football Association–approved ball must be:
- spherical;
- made of leather or other suitable material;
- of a circumference of not more than 28 inches (70 centimetres) and not less than 27 inches (68 centimetres);
- not more than 16 ounces (450 grams) in weight and not less than 14 ounces (410 grams) at the start of the match;
- of a pressure equal to 0.6–1.1 atmosphere (8.5–5.6 pounds/square inch or 600–1100 grams/centimetres square) at sea level.

Quickies
Did you know ...
- it is prohibited by the Laws of the Game for any logo other than FIFA's to appear on an regulation match ball?

Quickies
Did you know ...
- if a soccer ball is properly inflated it should bounce waist-high when dropped straight down from head height onto firm ground?

the reference "International Matchball Standard." Any of these markings show it to be an officially approved ball.

What happens if soccer a ball bursts during a game?

If a ball bursts or becomes otherwise defective during a match, the match must be stopped and, once a replacement ball is accepted by the referee, the match is restarted by dropping the replacement ball at the place where the original ball became defective. If the ball bursts or becomes defective while not in play at a kickoff, goal kick, corner kick, free kick, penalty kick, or throw-in, the ball is replaced before the match is restarted. The ball may not be changed without the authority of the referee.

Why do soccer balls have those multicoloured panels?

Ball spin is very important when playing soccer because it affects the direction of a ball's trajectory. The multicoloured panels make it easier to identify spin, and they are permitted by the Laws of the Game.

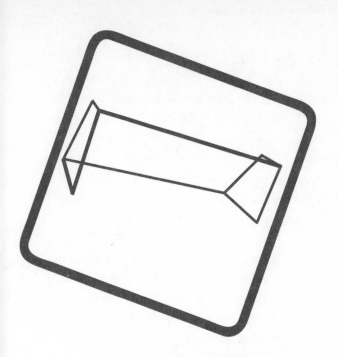

the world cup

Who was Jules Rimet?

Born in Haute-Saone in eastern France in 1876, Jules Rimet was the son of a poor grocer who migrated to Paris when Jules was 11 years old. He grew up to become a lawyer and in 1897, at young age of 24, he started a sports club in Paris called Red Star (today's Red Star Saint-Ouen, one of France's oldest soccer clubs). Rimet was instrumental in creating the world football body, the *Féderation Internationale de Football Association* (FIFA) in 1904. After the First Word War, in 1919, Rimet became the first president of the *Fédération Française de Football* (FFF) and, two years later, the head of the revived FIFA. As president of FIFA, he organized a vote in 1929 for the creation of a non-amateur international competition between FIFA member countries, which led to the first FIFA World Cup in 1930. Considered the founder of the FIFA World Cup tournament, Rimet remained president of FIFA for 33 years until 1954, taking the number of member countries from a dozen to 85.

Quickies
Did you know ...
• the first European country to win the World Cup was Italy, who won it at home in 1934?

What was the Jules Rimet trophy?

The original World Cup trophy was called "Victory." Designed by French sculptor Abel Lafleur, it stood 13.7 inches (35 centimetres) high and weighed approximately 8.4 pounds (3.8 kilograms). The statuette depicted Nike of Samothrace and was made of sterling silver and gold plate, with a blue base made of lapis lazuli. There was a gold plate on each of the four sides of the base, on which were engraved the name of the trophy as well as the names of the nine winners between 1930 and 1970. In 1946, it was renamed the Jules Rimet trophy in honour of the founder of the World Cup tournament.

How did Dr. Ottorino Barassi protect the Jules Rimet Cup?

During the Second World War, the Italian vice-president of FIFA, Dr.

Ottorino Barassi, hid the Jules Rimet Cup in a shoebox under his bed and thus saved it from falling into the hands of occupying troops.

Who was Pickles?

In 1966, the Jules Rimet Cup disappeared while on display at London's Westminster Central Hall, just a few months before the World Cup was due to take place in England. It was later found by a dog named Pickles, owned by a Thames river barge worker named David Corbett, wrapped in newspaper under a garden hedge in south London. Pickles and Corbett received £3,000 reward and England went on to win the cup.

World Cup Firsts
- First goal: Lucien Laurent (France) against Mexico, July 13, 1930.
- First penalty goal: Manuel Rocquetas Rosas (Mexico) against Argentina, July 19, 1930.
- First hat trick: Guillermo Stabile (Argentina) against Mexico, July 19, 1930.
- First player sent off: Mario de Las Casas (Peru) against Romania, July 14, 1930.
- First own goal: Ernst Loertscher (Switzerland) against West Germany, June 9, 1938.

What happened to the original Jules Rimet Cup?

If anyone knows, they aren't telling. In 1983, the original Jules Rimet Cup was stolen from a display at the Brazilian Football Confederation head-quarters in Rio de Janeiro, and it is believed that it was melted down by the thieves. The Brazilian Football Association, who had earned the right to keep the trophy in 1970 after having won it three times, ordered a replica from Eastman Kodak, who commissioned Wilhelm Geist and Son in Hanau, Germany, to recreate the trophy. Three Brazilians and an Argentine were arrested for the theft but released. Eventually they were tried and convicted in absentia.

Quickies
Did you know ...
- Hector Castro, who scored Uruguay's winning goal in the 1930 World Cup final, had only one hand?

Who created the World Cup Trophy used in today's competition?

When Brazil won the World Cup for the third time in 1970, according to the rules of the tournament, they took permanent possession of the Jules Rimet Cup. FIFA opened a competition to design a new trophy and Italian sculptor Silvio Gazzaniga won. His design beat out 53 submissions from seven nations. The new "FIFA World Cup" was cast by Italian trophy manufacturer Bertoni and features two athletes, back-to-back, with arms stretched upwards representing the moment of victory. A globe rests on their shoulders. The sculpture measures 14.2 inches (36 centimetres) high, is made of solid 18-carat gold and weighs 11 pounds (4.97 kilograms). It sits atop two rows of malachite, where the names of the winning nations are engraved. It can hold 17 names, which means it will be retired in 2038. Unlike the Rimet Cup, this trophy is FIFA's permanent property. Winning teams receive a gold-plated replica to keep.

Quickies

Did you know ...

- thirty-two teams qualify for the world cup from six regions — Africa, Asia, Europe, North America, Oceania, and South America — but only European and South American teams have ever won?

Why were there only four European teams in the first World Cup?

Because the Uruguayan government offered to pay all travel expenses, FIFA agreed to stage the first World Cup tournament in Uruguay. The decision was bitterly opposed by many European federations. Since there was no air travel in 1930, clubs would lose their players for almost three months as they sailed across the Atlantic and back again. As a result, only four European countries participated: France, Belgium, Romania, and Yugoslavia.

What was the lowest attendance for a World Cup match?

For a match between Romania and Peru in Montevideo on July 14, 1930, only 300 spectators attended.

Which team in World Cup 1930 was selected by their King?

For the inaugural World Cup championship in 1930, Romania's "football-crazy" King Carol II personally selected the players for his nation's team. At his request, each man was granted a three-month leave from their employers, with full pay. The Romanians won their first match, against Peru, but were knocked out in their second by Uruguay.

Teams with World Cup Titles
- Brazil: five wins
- Italy: four wins
- Germany: three wins
- Uruguay: two wins
- Argentina: two wins
- England: one win
- France: one win

Which teams competed in the first World Cup match?

France beat Mexico 4–1 in that match held in Montevideo, Uruguay, on July 13, 1930.

What did each Uruguayan player receive from the government after winning the World Cup in 1930?

The Uruguayan players came home national heroes, and each was presented by the municipality of Montevideo with a plot of land and new house.

Why was the match between Argentina and France on July 15, 1930, terminated six minutes early?

The referee had made a mistake. Brazilian referee Almeida Rego whistled to end the match at the 39th minute in the second half when Argentina was leading 1–0. He resumed the match half an hour later, but no goal was scored in the "extra" time.

Why did the American trainer have to be carried off during a 1930 World Cup semifinal against Argentina?

The American trainer ran onto the pitch to attend an injured player, but he dropped his medicine case and broke a bottle of chloroform. When he tried to pick it up, he breathed in the fumes and fell to the ground unconscious.

What was the first tied match in World Cup history?

That was when Italy and Spain came out 1–1 during the quarter-finals in Florence, Italy on May 31, 1934. The game was replayed on June 1 to a score of 1-0 for Italy, who eventually won the cup that year.

What was the first World Cup match with extra time?

The first World Cup match with extra time was played in Turin between Austria and France on May 27, 1934, to settle a 2–2 tie. Austria advanced to the quarter-finals.

What was the first World Cup final with extra time?

On June 10, 1934, Italy and Czechoslovakia played to a 1–1 tie in the World Cup final in Rome. Italy scored in extra time to win the cup.

Why did Austria did not appear in the 1938 World Cup, even though they qualified?

In Vienna on October 5, 1937, Austria qualified for the 1938 World Cup by defeating Latvia 2–1. But in March 1938, Nazi Germany annexed Austria in the Anschluss and the Austrian team was forced to withdraw. No team was offered the vacancy. Incidentally, the Nazi German team was eliminated in the first round by Switzerland.

> **Quickies**
> *Did you know ...*
> • in the 1930 World Cup final, Argentina's ball was used in the first half, which they won 2–1, and Uruguay's ball was used in the second half, which they won 3–0?

Why was Leonidas left out of the Brazilian team for the 1938 semifinal against Italy?

The Brazilian coach wanted to save Leonidas for the final. The decision not to field Leonidas in the semifinal was obviously wrong because Brazil unexpectedly lost 2–1 to Italy in the match. Ironically, in the third-place match two days later, Leonidas scored two goals and helped Brazil achieve a 4–2 victory over Sweden.

> **Quickies**
> *Did you know ...*
> • despite having to wear eyeglasses while playing, shortsighted Swiss centre-forward Poldi Kielholz scored three goals in two matches in the 1934 World Cup finals?

Why did England not play in the World Cup until 1950?

The four British FAs resigned from FIFA in February 1928 after a disagreement with how FIFA proposed to administer what are called "broken time payments" to amateur players in the Amsterdam Olympics that were being held that year. "Broken time payments" is the practice of a promoter or organizer compensating amateur players for lost income from their regular jobs. The British FAs had their own system in place and did not like FIFA's interference. They eventually rejoined FIFA in 1946, and participated in the World Cup for the first time in 1950.

Why did India once withdraw from the World Cup?

The team from India withdrew from the 1950 World Cup finals because FIFA would not permit them to play barefoot, as was their custom.

Why did Scotland decline to play in the 1950 World Cup finals?

As an incentive to bring the four British FAs back into its membership, FIFA announced that the 1949–1950 British Home Championship was to be used in Great Britain as a qualifying group for the 1950 World Cup, with the first- and second-place teams qualifying. England finished first and Scotland second in the Home Championship, but George Graham, secretary of the Scottish Football Association (SFA), had earlier declared that Scotland would only accept the FIFA invitation if the Scottish team was British champions. Thus, Scotland withdrew from the World Cup.

The Most Common Scores in World Cup Finals Matches
• 1–0:   128 matches
• 2–1:   101 matches
• 2–0:   79 matches

Why did Yugoslavia start their 1950 World Cup finals match against Brazil one player short?

Yugoslavian player Rajko Mitic hit his head on an iron girder as he was leaving the dressing room. The referee refused to delay the game, so Yugoslavia kicked off with 10 men. By the time the heavily bandaged Mitic joined his teammates, Yugoslavia was already down one goal.

What was the first World Cup mascot?

The first World Cup mascot was a lion-like boy called Willie used for the England 1966 World Cup.

What was the highest attendance for a World Cup final?

There's agreement on the match, but not on the number. The BBC reports that 199,854 spectators attended the World Cup final between Brazil and Uruguay at Estádio do Maracanã, in Rio de Janeiro on July 16, 1950. But FIFA officially records the number at 174,000. Either way, it stands as a record attendance.

When did the tradition of swapping shirts begin in World Cup?

The shirt-swapping tradition began in 1954. Shirt swapping was once officially prohibited in 1986 because FIFA did not want players to bare their chests on the field.

Who was Andy Beattie?

Scotland qualified for the World Cup in 1954. The team manager was a former professional player named Andy Beattie. Scotland's tournament was something of a farce. While the rules allowed for a squad of 22, out of frugality, a team of only 13 men made the trip to Switzerland, where the tournament was being held. In addition, the team had to provide their own equipment. The squad included no members from the Rangers, one of Scotland's top teams, because they were on tour in the United States. Scotland lost their first match 0–1 against Austria. Frustrated by the amateurishness of it all, Beattie announced during his pre-game speech for the second match that he was resigning. The Scots lost that game, against Uruguay, 0–7, and were knocked out of competition. Player Tommy Dochery later quipped, "We were lucky to get nil."

Quickies

Did you know ...

- the 1958 World Cup marked the debut on the world stage of 17-year-old Pelé?

How many players have scored in four successive finals tournaments?

Only two: Both Pelé of Brazil and Uwe Seeler of West Germany scored in the finals of 1958, 1962, 1966, and 1970.

Who was the youngest player to score in the World Cup finals?

That would be none other than Pelé, who was 17 years and 239 days old when he scored for Brazil against Wales to win a quarter-final match 1–0 on June 19, 1958. Brazil went on to win the tournament and Pelé still holds the record for youngest player to have played for a World Cup champion team.

Why was attendance at the 1958 World Cup playoff match between Wales and Hungary exceptionally low?

On June 16, 1958, the Soviet-backed Hungarian People's Republic executed former Hungarian prime minister Imre Nagy, along with high-ranking Hungarian freedom fighter Pál Maléter. The following day, the Hungarian national soccer team faced Wales at the Råsunda Stadium, in Solna, Sweden. Despite a stadium capacity of 35,000, only 2,823 spectators were in attendance, as people boycotted the match to show their sympathy for the Hungarian rebellion.

> **Quickies**
> *Did you know ...*
> • the 1966 World Cup opening match between England and Uruguay was delayed because seven English players had forgotten their identity cards at their hotel? A police motorcyclist was sent to collect them.

What was "The Soccer War"?

The Soccer War, also known as the 100-hours War, was a five-day war between El Salvador and Honduras in 1969. It was caused by political conflicts between the two nations, namely issues concerning immigration from El Salvador to Honduras. Tensions boiled over into rioting at two qualifying matches between the nations for the 1970 World Cup, on June 8 and 15. Many people erroneously believe the war was a result of these soccer riots, but the truth was the opposite. The riots resulted from earlier tensions; indeed, by July 14, the Salvadoran air force had begun launching attacks into Honduras. The conflict lasted until a ceasefire was arranged on July 18, leaving 6,000 dead and 12,000 wounded.

> **The Most Frequent Number of Goals in World Cup Final Matches**
> • 3 goals: 142 matches
> • 2 goals: 148 matches
> • 1 goal: 128 matches

Why did El Salvador intentionally kick the ball into the crowd at a World Cup match?

Shortly before halftime at a first-round game against Mexico in the 1970

World Cup, a free kick was awarded to El Salvador, but a Mexican player mistakenly took the kick and passed the ball to his teammate Valdivia. To everyone's surprise, referee Hussain Kandil let play continue. Valdivia scored off the pass, and the goal was allowed. When their appeals were denied by Kandil, the El Salvador players restarted the game by kicking the ball into the crowd.

What is the highest attendance for a World Cup qualifying match?

Quickies
Did you know ...
• upon returning to his hotel after his team's defeat in the quarter-finals in the 1970 World Cup, disappointed English player Alan Ball threw his tournament medal out his room window?

On August 31, 1969, a record 183,341 spectators paid to watch Brazil defeat Paraguay 1–0 in a World Cup qualifying match at Estádio do Maracanã in Rio de Janeiro. Brazil went on to win the World Cup.

In which finals was a substitute first used?

The first substitute in World Cup finals was Soviet player Anatoly Puzach, who replaced Viktor Serebrannikov at the 45-minute mark of the opening match against Mexico on May 31, 1970. Before 1970, only injured players were allowed to be replaced.

By what unusual method did Chile qualify for the 1973 World Cup finals in a match against the USSR?

Quickies
Did you know ...
• Brazilian player Tostao gave his 1970 World Cup winners' medal to a surgeon who had performed two operations on his eye before the finals?

Quite simply, by kicking the ball into an undefended net. Earlier in the year, after a *coup d'état* by General Augusto Pinochet, thousands of supporters of Marxist

Chilean President Allende had been executed in the National Stadium in Santiago. Out of protest, the USSR refused to play in the stadium and the match was held without Soviet players present. The Chilean players kicked off the game and scored into the empty Soviet net. Then the game was abandoned and awarded to Chile. As a result, Chile automatically qualified for the 1974 finals but were eliminated in the first round.

Which was the first sub-Saharan African nation to play in a World Cup finals?

When Zaire qualified for the 1974 finals, they became the first sub-Saharan African nation to advance beyond the qualifying stage into the finals. The Zairean president promised each player a house, a car, and free holidays. All of these offers were withdrawn when Zaire lost all three matches, scored no goals, and gave up 14 goals.

Which country has participated in every World Cup qualifying competition but never made it through to the finals?

From 1934 to 2005, Luxembourg played 104 qualifying matches and lost 100, scoring 50 goals and giving up 356. The only two teams that Luxembourg has defeated in qualifiers are Portugal (4–2 on October 8, 1961) and Turkey (2–0 on October 22, 1972) — not quite good enough to get them in.

Why was start of the 1974 World Cup final delayed?

The referee found that all the corner and centre-line flag-posts were missing as Holland and West Germany lined up for the kickoff to the 1974 final in Munich. Match officials had forgotten to put the flags back in after the opening ceremony.

What controversy surrounded Welsh referee Clive Thomas?

On June 3, 1978, as the clock wound down in the first-round finals match between Brazil and Sweden in the 1978 World Cup, Brazil's Zico headed a corner kick into the Swedish net. But Thomas disallowed the goal because he had whistled to end the match while the ball was in the air. The final score stayed at 1–1.

Why was Prince Fahid, the Kuwaiti FA president, fined US$14,000 after a 1982 World Cup finals match against France?

After France scored, one of the Kuwaiti players complained to Soviet referee Miroslav Stupar that prior to the goal he'd heard a whistle-stopping play. When Prince Fahid walked out onto the field to argue the point with the referee and threatened to pull out his team, Stupar reversed his goal decision. France ended up winning the match anyway, 4–1. For their actions, Stupar was suspended and Fahid fined.

What was the first World Cup match decided on a penalty shootout?

A semifinal match on July 8, 1982, between West Germany and France had to be settled with the first shootout in World Cup history. Germany won the shootout 5–4, but lost in the finals to Italy.

Who was the youngest player to appear in the World Cup finals?

Norman Whiteside who was 17 years and 42 days old when he played for Northern Ireland against Yugoslavia on June 17, 1982. The group-round match, played at La Romareda stadium, in Zaragoza, Spain, came out a draw. Whiteside was the only player in the match to receive a caution.

Who was the oldest player to play for a World Cup champion team?

Dino Zoff, the goalkeeper and captain of Italy's team, was the oldest World Cup champion at the age of 40 when he played in the 1982 final.

Why did Scotland's coach Jack Stein have to be replaced after a 1986 World Cup qualifier against Wales?

He died. Jack Stein suffered a heart attack after Scotland's 1–1 tie in Wales on September 10, 1985. Alex Ferguson took over the job, and led Scotland to qualify for Mexico in 1986.

What is the most common score of a penalty shootout in World Cup finals?

The penalty shootout was introduced in 1982. Between then and 2006, there have been 16 penalty shootouts in World Cup finals matches. The most common result is the score of 4–3, with five shootouts ending so. Germany has won all four of their shootouts. Belgium has never missed any of their attempts.

Quickies

Did you know ...

• Colombia was originally selected to host the 1986 World Cup, but they lacked the funds to bring their soccer facilities up to FIFA's standards? Mexico replaced Colombia as the 1986 host country.

Why was Chilean goalkeeper Roberto Rojas banned for life by FIFA?

On September 3, 1989, Brazil was leading 1–0 with 23 minutes left in a decisive World Cup qualifier against Chile at the Maracana Stadium in Rio de Janeiro. In an attempt to disqualify the match, the Chilean goalkeeper Roberto Rojas pretended to have been hit and seriously injured by a flare thrown from the Brazilian crowd. The whole Chilean team walked off in protest, and the match was abandoned. Investigations by the Chilean Soccer Federation and FIFA concluded that he had faked the injury. FIFA awarded Brazil a 2–0 victory, banned Rojas from international play for life and banned Chile from the 1994 World Cup.

Who was the oldest player to appear in the World Cup finals?

Quickies
Did you know ...
- Mexico was banned from participating in the 1990 World Cup because they had deliberately fielded three over-age players in a FIFA international youth tournament?

In a match against Russia on June 28, 1994, Cameroon's forward Roger Milla, a substitute who came on the 45-minute mark, was 42 years and 39 days old. That first-round match, played at Stanford Stadium, Palo Alto, California, was won by Russia 6–1. Milla scored Cameroon's only goal, also becoming the oldest player to score in the World Cup finals.

Why did an Albanian coach ask his players not to swap shirts after a World Cup qualifying match?

They were broke. Not the shirts, that is, but the Albanians. It is traditional in such contests for teams to swap jerseys, but the Albanian team was so financially beleaguered that they did not even have a full complement of shirts before the match against Spain on September 22, 1993. Albanian coach Bekjush Birce wanted to save the shirts for the next match.

What good-luck charm did Belgium goalkeeper Michel Preud'homme abandon in World Cup 1994?

For good luck, Preud'homme always wore the shirt of Standard Liège, his first soccer club, beneath his national jersey during international matches. He had to abandon this tradition in the United States because of the heat in Orlando, Florida. Belgium's luck officially ran out in the knockout stage, where they lost to Germany.

The Four Countries That Have Hosted the World Cup Twice

- Mexico: 1938 and 1986
- Italy: 1934 and 1990
- France: 1938 and 1998
- Germany: 1974 (West Germany) and 2006 (unified Germany)

What was the first World Cup final decided on penalty shootout?

After a tie of 0–0 in the 1994 World Cup final between Brazil and Italy, a shootout had to be used for the first time to settle the tournament. Brazil won, 3–2.

Why was German player Stefan Effenberg sent home early from the World Cup in 1994?

On June 24, 1994, while playing a World Cup group game against South Korea at the Cotton Bowl in Dallas, German midfielder Stefan Effenberg not only received a yellow card but was also ejected from the tournament — by his own coach! Coming off the field for a substitute, Effenberg flipped the bird to raucous, jeering fans. Seeing this, German coach Berti Vogts dropped Effenberg from the tournament and sent him packing back to Germany.

Quickies

Did you know ...

- when Italian striker Gianfranco Zola was sent off in a knockout stage match against Nigeria in the 1994 World Cup, it would be the only time in his career that he would be shown the red card? It was also his 28th birthday.

What was the lowest attendance for a World Cup qualifying match?

On May 7, 2001, only 20 spectators turned up to watch Turkmenistan's 1–0 victory over Chinese Taipei in Amman. Neither team has ever made it to the finals.

What was "Fadiga's necklace"?

In the lead-up to 2002 World Cup finals, Senegalese midfielder Khalilou Fadiga was accused of stealing a necklace from a jewellery shop in Korea. The Korean police dropped charges at the request of the shop owner, who displayed the necklace, worth US$240, in his shop window, calling it "Fadiga's necklace."

On the day of the 2002 World Cup final between Germany and Brazil in Japan, why did the teams for Montserrat and Bhutan also meet?

On that day, Montserrat ranked 203rd, and Bhutan ranked 202nd, and were the lowest-ranked teams in the world. It was decided that the two would meet for a friendly contest, and the Montserrat team travelled five days from their tiny Caribbean island to the Himalayan kingdom of Bhutan. Bhutan won 4–0 in front of a crowd of 15,000.

What did Brazilian player Ronaldino donate to charity during World Cup 2006?

Two locks of his hair. They were donated for an auction organized by a Swiss newspaper to raise fund for a cancer charity. The hair was collected by a team of Swiss barbers in the Brazilian camp in Switzerland before the start of the finals.

Quickies
Did you know ...
• prior to the 2006 World Cup a Shamanic priest from Ecuador named Tzamarenda Naychapi came to Germany to purify the stadiums where Ecuador would play? The spell apparently only lasted until the second round, when they were eliminated after losing to England 1–0.

Who were "The Elephants"?

Ivory Coast's team — nicknamed "The Elephants" — created their own "elephant dance" and practised the steps in training sessions before each match of the 2006 World Cup, hoping to dance before cheering fans to celebrate a winning goal. They lost their first two group matches, but the world had the chance to watch them dance on June 21, 2006, when they defeated Serbia and Montenegro 3–2.

What mistake did British referee Graham Poll make that led to his expulsion from World Cup 2006?

In a group match between Australia and Croatia on June 22, 2006, Graham Poll showed Josip Simunic three yellow cards before sending him off. The limit for yellow-card cautions is two. In an earlier match between Togo and South Korea on June 13, 2006, Poll had also given Togo captain Jean-Paul Abalo a red card before a yellow. FIFA expelled him from the tournament.

Six Teams That Won the World Cup While Hosting the Tournament
• Uruguay (1930)
• Italy (1934)
• England (1966)
• West Germany (1974)
• Argentina (1978)
• France (1998)

What country holds the record for the longest winless streak in the World Cup?

That would be Bulgaria, with 6 ties and 11 losses in 17 consecutive matches from 1962 to 1994.

What country holds the record for the longest goalless streak in the World Cup?

That would be Bolivia, with a five-match goal drought from 1930 to 1994.

What country holds the record for the longest winning streak in the World Cup?

That would be Brazil, with seven matches in 2002 and four in 2006 for a record total of 11 straight wins.

What country holds the record for the longest losing streak in the World Cup?

That would be Mexico, with nine consecutive losses from 1930 to 1958.

domestics
and internationals

What was the first tournament played between all four national teams of the United Kingdom?

In the early 1880s, the football associations of England, Scotland, Wales, and Ireland each had slightly different rules for the game. When friendly matches were played, the rules of the hosting team were used. On December 6, 1882, the four associations met in Manchester and agreed on one uniform set of rules. This meeting not only marked the founding of the International Football Association Board (IFAB), but also gave birth to the British Home Championship, which would see the four national "Home Teams" — England, Scotland, Wales, and Ireland — compete in a formal tournament played out over the 1883–84 season. The winner was Scotland.

What was the Ibrox Disaster of 1902?

For the final of the 1902 British Home Championship, over 68,000 fans gathered at Ibrox Park in Glasgow on April 5 to watch Scotland face England. In the first half, shortly before 4:00 p.m., a section of terrace in the stadium's West Stand collapsed, killing 25 and injuring over 500. Play was stopped, but was restarted after 20 minutes. The match played out to a 1–1 draw, but was later declared void and replayed on May 2 at Villa Park, Birmingham, to a 2–2 draw.

British Home Championship Winners				
Country:	England	Scotland	Wales	Ireland/ North Ireland
Outright Wins:	34	24	7	3
Shared Two-way:	14	11	3	2
Shared Three-ways:	5	5	1	2
Shared Three-ways:	1	1	1	1
Total:	54	41	12	8

Why was the British Home Championship not completed in 1981?

The British Home Championship was a contest between the four national "Home Teams" of Great Britain — England, Scotland, Wales, and Ireland. From 1915 to 1919, and from 1940 to 1946, the Championship was not contested due to the First and Second World Wars. Aside from those years, the tournament was contested each soccer season in Great Britain over the space of a century, from 1883–84 to 1983–84, when it was officially discontinued. But in the 1980–81 season, although the tournament was started, it was not completed. The championship was scheduled to be played in May 1981; however, on May 5, the IRA hunger-strike leader Bobby Sands died in the Maze Prison, invoking a storm of protest and anti-British feeling in the province. The English and Welsh FAs, whose teams were scheduled to play at Windsor Park, in Belfast, later in the month, declined to play, thus rendering the Championship incomplete and void.

> **Quickies**
> *Did you know ...*
> • for the first and only time in the 100 years of the British Home Championship, in 1956 all four teams finished even, with three points each, and so shared the cup?

What was the *Torneo Internazionale Stampa Sportiva*?

This was one of the earliest international soccer tournaments. Held in Turin, Italy, in 1908, and organized by Italian sports magazine *La Stampa Sportiva*, the *Torneo Internazionale* featured club teams from Italy, France, Switzerland, and Germany. Swiss team Servette FC were the eventual winners, beating Torino 3–1 in the final on April 20.

Who was Sir Thomas Lipton?

Aside from being a sea merchant who gave the world Lipton Tea, Scotsman Sir Thomas Lipton also gave the world what is sometimes described as "The First World Cup," when he sponsored the Sir Thomas Lipton Trophy tournament in Turin in 1909 and 1911. The Lipton tournament was a championship between individual clubs (not national teams) from different nations, each one of which represented an entire nation. The competition featured the most prestigious professional clubs from Italy, Germany, and Switzerland, but England's FA refused to be associated with the competition and declined the offer to send a professional team. Lipton invited West Auckland, an amateur side from County Durham, to represent England instead. West Auckland won the first tournament and returned in 1911 to successfully defend their title, and was given the trophy to keep forever as per the rules of the competition.

What is Nasazzi's Baton?

José Nasazzi is regarded by many as Uruguay's greatest-ever soccer player. Known as *"El Gran Mariscal"* (The Great Marshal), he had already won the gold medal at the 1924 and 1928 Olympic Games, as well as the *Copa América* in 1923, 1924, and 1926, by the time he led Uruguay to victory at the first World Cup in 1930. Named after the great Uruguayan, the Nasazzi Baton, which is maintained by the Rec.Sport.Soccer Statistics Foundation, is an unofficial system of designating a "fantasy" world soccer champion team. The Nasazzi Baton changes hands, figuratively speaking, whenever the current world champion is defeated, but only in matches regarded by FIFA and both participating teams as a full international. For example, if Canada wins the 2010 World Cup, they take the Nasazzi Baton because they have become reigning world champions, but then the baton, and unofficial championship, is passed to the first team to beat Canada after the World Cup, and so on. Knockout tournaments that are decided by extra time, penalty kicks, golden goals, silver goals, corner kicks, tossing a coin, or drawing lots are regarded as drawn matches — the Baton does not change hands.

What are the Unofficial Football World Championships?

In the 1966–67 British Home Championship, England was fresh from victory at the 1966 World Cup and were favourites to win the tournament. But when Scotland emerged victorious from the Home Championship final at Wembley Stadium in London on April 15, jubilant Scottish fans jokingly declared Scotland the "World Champions," since the game was England's first defeat since winning the World Cup. This joke ultimately led to the creation of a website called the "Unofficial Football World Championships," on which soccer fans follow this fictional championship title using a knockout system similar to that used in boxing.

What is the oldest trophy in soccer?

The Scottish Cup was made in Glasgow by George Edwards and Sons of Buchanan Street and, having been minted in 1885, is the oldest national trophy in world soccer.

Which teams played in the first Scottish Cup final?

The Scottish Cup, or as it is formally known, the Scottish Football Association Challenge Cup, started in the 1873–74 season, and was contested by 16 teams that year. The trophy was first awarded to Queen's Park when they defeated fellow Glasgow club Clydesdale 2–0 in the final in front of 3,000 fans at First Hampden Park on March 21, 1874.

What is the biggest victory in Scottish Cup competition?

In 1885, the Orion Cricket Club was mistakenly invited to enter the Scottish Cup instead of Orion FC, an Aberdeen soccer club. On September 12 that year, under the name Bon Accord, Orion Cricket's

Quickies

Did you know ...

• the first Old Firm final in the Scottish Cup was played in 1894 and saw Rangers defeat Celtic 3–1?

grossly inexperienced players faced off against Arbroath FC, a team that had been together for seven years. The match has gone down in history for yielding the biggest victory in Scottish Cup competition as Arbroath ran circles around Bon Accord to tally a 36–0 victory. A single Arbroath play, John Petrie, scored 13 goals in the match.

What is the second-biggest victory in Scottish Cup competition?

In the first round of the 1885 Scottish Cup, Dundee Harp were met by Aberdeen Rovers on their home pitch. Witnessing one of the most lopsided victories in Scottish Cup competition, the referee for the match noted 37 goals for Dundee, and 0 for Aberdeen. At the end of the match, however, Harp's secretary had recorded only 35 goals for his side, so it was agreed the lower number would be sent to the Scottish Football Association as the official score. If only that secretary had known he was denying his team a record by one point! For on the very same day, September 12, just 18 miles (29 kilometres) away, Arbroath FC had set a record for the biggest victory in Scottish Cup competition, defeating Bon accord 36–0.

Why was the Scottish Cup of 1909 never decided?

On April 10, 1909, the "Old Firm" Glasgow rivals — Rangers and Celtic — met in the final of the Scottish Cup playing to a 2–2 draw at Hampden Park. A replay was scheduled for April 17, but rumours began to spread through the city that the Scottish Football Association had fixed the final so that the lucrative replay could be staged. When the replay itself also came out in a draw, of 1–1, and the 60,000 fans in attendance discovered that SFA rules stipulated that extra time could only be added to a *second* replay, a riot ensued. Fans tore up the pitch, pulled down goalposts and set parts of the stadium on fire. Mounted police were called in but could not stop the rioters from spilling out into the city centre. Days later, after the dust settled, both teams petitioned the SFA to abandon the tie. The SFA complied and the final went undecided that year.

> **Quickies**
> *Did you know ...*
> • with their win of the 1928 Scottish Cup, Rangers ended a 25-year Cup jinx?

What is the record attendance for a Scottish Cup final?

The record attendance for a Scottish Cup final was set April 24, 1937, when, by official counts, 146,433 spectators saw Celtic beat Aberdeen 2–1 at Glasgow's Hampden Park.

What was the Scottish War Emergency Cup?

The Scottish War Emergency Cup was a temporary competition held at the start of the Second World War, due to the suspension of the Scottish Cup by the SFA. It was held between February and May in 1940, and the competition was open to all league clubs still operating at the time. Rangers beat Dundee United 1–0 in the final on May 4 at Hampden Park and to this day display the cup in their trophy room.

> **Only four clubs have won the Scottish Cup three times in succession.***
> • Queen's Park (1874, 1875, 1876)
> • Vale of Leven (1877, 1878, 1879)
> • Rangers (1934, 1935, 1936)
> • Aberdeen (1982, 1983, 1984)
> *None have won it four times.

What was the Southern League Cup?

The Southern Football League was a regional Scottish league set up in 1940 after the Scottish Football League decided to suspend national competition for the duration of the war. The Southern League Cup was a competition held annually from 1940 to 1946 between the 16 teams of the temporary league. After the war, the Southern League Cup became Scottish League Cup.

Have any teams outside the Irish Football League ever won the Irish Cup?

Since the inception of the Irish Football League in 1890–91, the Irish Cup has been won by Irish League teams on every occasion except three famous "giant-killing" occasions when junior teams beat senior opponents in the final: In 1928, Willowfield beat Larne 1–0; in 1955, Dundela beat Glenavon 3–0; and in 1976, Carrick Rangers beat Linfield 2–1.

Quickies
Did you know ...
- the Irish Cup began in 1881 and is the fourth-oldest national cup competition in the world?

What team holds the record for consecutive wins of the Irish Cup?

Glentoran FC, which was founded in 1882 and plays in the IFA Premiership at The Oval in Belfast, hold the record for the most consecutive wins of the Irish Cup, with four victories from 1985 to 1988. Glentoran was also the first Irish team to win a European trophy, taking the Vienna Cup in 1914.

Quickies
Did you know ...
- the record for consecutive Irish League championship titles is six, held jointly by Belfast Celtic FC (1935–40 and 1947–48) and Linfield FC (1981–87)?

Why was the 1920 Irish Cup awarded without a final being played?

In the 1920 Irish Cup competition, Shelbourne FC, who had beaten Glenavon FC in one semifinal, were awarded the cup without playing the final, when the two other semifinalists, Glentoran FC and Belfast Celtic FC, were both disqualified — Glentoran for fielding an unlisted player, Belfast Celtic after one of their supporters fired gunshots at the Glentoran fans.

Who won the first Welsh Cup?

The first Welsh Cup was played in 1878, with Wrexham FC defeating Ruabon Druids in the final 1–0. Founded in 1872, Wrexham is the oldest professional club in Wales and holds the record for most Welsh Cup wins, with 23.

> **Quickies**
> *Did you know ...*
> • Llansantffraid FC were the first club to win the Welsh Cup in a penalty shootout, defeating Barry Town 3–2 on penalties after coming to a 3–3 draw at National Stadium, Cardiff, May 19, 1996?

Why are Wales' three historically strongest teams now barred from competing for the Welsh Cup?

Wrexham, Cardiff City, and Swansea City are teams in a kind of limbo. Professional teams from northern Wales, all three have been playing within the English Football League since before the formation in 1992 of the League of Wales by the Football Association of Wales. Prior to 1992, any FAW member team could compete for the Welsh Cup, and Wrexham, Cardiff, and Swansea had collectively garnered 55 championships since the cup's founding in 1878. But with the formation of the new Welsh league, English league teams were excluded from Welsh Cup competition, leaving Wrexham, Cardiff City, and Swansea City out in the cold.

Number of Wins of the Welsh Cup By Team

- Wrexham — 23
- Cardiff City — 22
- Swansea City (including Swansea Town) — 10
- Druids — 8
- Barry Town, Shrewsbury Town, Bangor City (including Bangor) — 6
- Chirk AAA — 5
- Rhyl — 4
- Chester, Merthyr Tydfil, Wellington Town — 3
- Crewe Alexandra, Oswestry United FC, Total Network Solutions (including Llansantffraid) — 2
- Aberystwyth, Borough United, Bristol City, Carmarthen Town, Connah's Quay and Shotton, Ebbw Vale, Fflint Town United, Hereford United, Inter Cable-Tel Cardiff, Lovell's Athletic, Newport County, Newtown, Newtown White Stars, Oswestry White Stars, South Liverpool, Tranmere Rovers — 1

Why are the Welsh teams Wrexham, Cardiff City, and Swansea City barred from competing for the UEFA Cup?

Since long before the formation in 1992 of the League of Wales, the Welsh teams Wrexham, Cardiff City, and Swansea City have competed within the English Football League, striving annually to get to the FA Cup. In 1995, the Union of European Football Associations (UEFA), barred any Welsh team playing outside its own nation's league from competing for the UEFA cup. The reasoning was that, if Wrexham, Cardiff, or Swansea were to win the FA Cup, since the winners of both the FA Cup and the Welsh Cup are each guaranteed a spot in the UEFA Cup, Wales could potentially see two teams go to the UEFA Cup.

What is the League Cup?

The League Cup is an annual knockout competition open to the twenty clubs of England's FA Premier League, and the 72 clubs of England's Football League, which organizes the competition. It was first played in the 1961, seeing Aston Villa emerge victorious over Rotherham United in a two-leg final. Since 1982, the competition has taken its name from a sponsor and is currently called the Carling Cup.

Quickies

Did you know ...

- the winners of the Carling Cup are guaranteed a UEFA Cup slot, making England one of only two nations to offer qualification for Europe to its second cup competition winners? The other is France.

Why was the League Cup begun?

During the late 1950s, the majority of senior English clubs equipped their grounds with floodlights. This opened up the opportunity to hold games on weekday evenings throughout the winter. The League Cup was introduced in the 1960–61 season specifically as a mid-week floodlit tournament. In the early years, many of the top teams declined to take part. It was only when automatic entry to the UEFA Cup was promised to the winners that the full league membership took part.

Since 1982, the League Cup has been named after its sponsor, giving it the following names:
- Milk Cup (1981–82 to 1985–86), sponsored by the Milk Marketing Board;
- Littlewoods Challenge Cup (1986–87 to 1989–90), sponsored by Littlewoods;
- Rumbelows Cup (1990–91 and 1991–92), sponsored by Rumbelows;
- Coca-Cola Cup (1992–93 to 1997–98), sponsored by Coca-Cola;
- Worthington Cup (1998–99 to 2002–03), sponsored by Worthington Draught bitter;
- Carling Cup (2003–04 to present), sponsored by Carling.

Which teams played in the first FA Cup final?

The first FA Cup Final took place at Kennington Oval, London, on Saturday, March 16, 1872, before a crowd of 2,000. At the time, soccer matches were played without crossbars or goalnets. There were also no free kicks or penalties and the pitch markings did not include a centre-circle or a halfway line. The Wanderers defeated the Royal Engineers 1–0 on a goal from A.H. Chequer.

Quickies
Did you know ...
- the first team to successfully defend the League Cup championship was Nottingham Forest when they beat Liverpool and Southampton in 1978 and 1979 respectively?

Quickies
Did you know ...
- in 1993, when Arsenal won the first-ever League Cup/FA Cup double, they faced Sheffield Wednesday FC in the final at both tournaments?

What was the "Little Tin Idol"?

The original FA Cup trophy, awarded from 1872 to 1895, was made by Martin, Hall and Co. and looked nothing like the one played for today. Made of silver, it was less than 18 inches (45 centimetres) high and cost £20 to make. It had a figure of a footballer on the top and was popularly known as the "Little Tin Idol." In 1895, it was stolen from the William Shillcock football outfitters shop in Newtown Row, Birmingham, and never recovered.

Who was Harry Burge?

In 1958, 83-year-old Harry Burge, who lived in a Birmingham hostel for the homeless, confessed to a reporter from a British newspaper that he was the thief who stole the original FA Cup trophy, the "Little Tin Idol." He claimed to have melted it down to make counterfeit half-crown coins.

Why was the second FA Cup trophy withdrawn?

In 1910 The FA discovered that the second FA Cup trophy, which had been in circulation since 1896, was based on a pirated design so they withdrew the trophy and presented it to Lord Kinnaird to mark his 21 years as FA President.

What double link does Bradford City have to the third FA Cup trophy?

The third FA Cup trophy was designed in 1910 by the firm of Messrs. Fattorini and Sons of Bradford. In an amazing coincidence, Bradford City AFC were the first winners of the new trophy in 1911.

When did the tradition of tying coloured ribbons to the FA Cup trophy begin?

When Tottenham Hotspur FC won the FA Cup In 1901, at the celebration dinner they decided to decorate the trophy and tied ribbons on its handle in the colours of their club (in their case, blue and white). Every team since has similarly decorated the trophy with their own colours.

When was the first FA Cup final played at Empire Stadium, Wembley?

The first FA Cup final at Empire Stadium, Wembley, was played on the stadium's opening day, April 28, 1923. Before the match a crowd of 100,000 people rushed the gates, bursting the barriers and swarming onto the pitch. About 200,000 people squeezed into a space meant to accommodate 127,000, and it took three-quarters of an hour for mounted police to clear the field before play could begin. As King George V looked on from the Royal Box, Bolton Wanderers defeated West Ham United 2–0.

Division of the FA Cup Purse

- Extra Preliminary Round winners (129)   £500
- Preliminary Round winners (166)   £1,000
- First Round Qualifying winners (116)   £2,250
- Second Round Qualifying winners (80)   £3,750
- Third Round Qualifying winners (40)   £5,000
- Fourth Round Qualifying winners (32)   £10,000
- First Round winners (40)   £16,000
- Second Round winners (20)   £24,000
- Third Round winners (32)   £40,000
- Fourth Round winners (16)   £60,000
- Fifth Round winners (8)   £120,000
- Sixth Round winners (4)   £300,000
- Semifinal winners (2)   £900,000
- Winners (1)   £1,000,000

Have any teams from outside England ever won the FA Cup?

Only once. Because the Football Association of Wales did not have its own league until 1992, the Welsh team Cardiff City have long played in the English Football League. In 1927 they made it to the FA Cup Final, defeating Arsenal 1–0 at Wembley Stadium on Saturday, April 23. The lone goal in the match came in the 73rd minute, when Cardiff striker Hughie Ferguson — a Scotsman — netted the ball past Arsenal goalkeeper Dan Lewis — a Welshman.

When was the first period of extra time in an FA Cup final?

The first period of extra time in an FA Cup final was played between the Royal Engineers and Old Etonians on March 13, 1875. It didn't settle their 1–1 draw, so the match was replayed March 16, with the Engineers winning 2–0.

FA Cup Finals Decided by Replays
- 1875 — Royal Engineers defeats Old Etonians 2–0
- 1876 — Wanderers defeats Old Etonians 3–0
- 1886 — Blackburn Rover defeats West Bromwich Albion 2–0
- 1901 — Tottenham Hotspur defeats Sheffield United 3–1
- 1902 — Sheffield United defeats Southhampton 2–1
- 1910 — Newcastle United defeats Barnsley 2–0
- 1911 — Bradford City defeats Newcastle United 1–0
- 1912 — Barnsely defeats West Bromwich Albion 1–0
- 1970 — Chelsea defeats Leeds 2–1
- 1981 — Tottenham Hotspur defeats Manchester City 3–2
- 1982 — Tottenham Hotspur defeats Queens Park Rangers 1–0
- 1983 — Manchester United defeats Brighton and Hove Albion 4–0
- 1990 — Manchester United defeats Crystal Palace 1–0
- 1993 — Arsenal defeats Sheffield Wednesday 2–1 aet

How did the FA Cup help give the world windshield wipers?

In April 1908, Newcastle United FC's official team photographer, Gladstone Adams, drove down from Newcastle upon Tyne to London in a 1904 Darracq-Caron motorcar to see his team playing in the FA Cup final at Wembley Stadium. Newcastle lost the match, held April 25, to Wolverhampton Wanderers FC, 3–1. During Adams's trip home, snow began to fall and he had to keep stopping to clear his windscreen. It was during this snowstorm that he had a brainstorm leading him to invent the windshield wiper, which he patented in 1911.

Top Ten FA Cup Winners
- Manchester United: 11 wins in 18 appearance
- Arsenal: 10 wins in 17 appearances
- Tottenham Hotspur: 8 wins in 9 appearances
- Aston Villa: 7 wins in 10 appearances
- Liverpool: 7 wins in 13 appearances
- Blackburn Rovers: 6 wins in 8 appearances
- Newcastle United: 6 wins in 13 appearances
- Everton: 5 wins in 12 appearances
- The Wanderers: 5 wins in 5 appearance
- West Bromwich Albion: 5 wins in 10 appearances

Who was the oldest player to appear in an FA Cup final?

Billy Hampson who played for Newcastle United FC, played in the 1924 FA Cup final against Aston Villa at aged 41 years 257 days. His team took the day, winning 2–0, making Hampson also the oldest FA Cup champion player. He retired at 47.

What was the first non-English team in the FA Cup final?

In 1884, Glasgow's Queen's Park FC became the first club from outside England to reach the FA Cup final. They lost to Blackburn Rovers, 2–1. They did it again in 1885, and lost it again to Blackburn Rovers, 2–0.

What was the Cup Winner's Cup?

The UEFA Cup Winners' Cup was a soccer-club competition contested annually by the winners of all European domestic cup competitions. From its inception until 1994, it was known as the European Cup Winners' Cup. The first competition was held in the 1960–61 season, with AFC Florentina emerging victorious, and the last was in 1998–99, with SS Lazio taking the final. The competition was then abolished after 1999 to make way for a further expansion to the UEFA Champions League.

What was the Cup Winners' Cup jinx?

In the 39 years that the Cup Winners' Cup was staged, although a number of clubs won the trophy more than once, no club ever successfully defended the championship two years running. As a result, a superstition called the "CWC Jinx" was embraced, postulating that Cup Winners' Cup champions were jinxed to lose the competition the next year.

> **Cup Winners' Cup Champions Beaten by the CWC Jinx**
> - Florentina wins 1961 final, loses 1962 final.
> - AC Milan wins 1973 final, loses 1974 final.
> - Anderlecht wins 1976 final, loses 1977 final.
> - Ajax wins 1987 final, loses 1988 final.
> - Parma wins 1993 final, loses 1994 final.
> - Arsenal wins 1994 final, loses 1995 final.
> - Paris Saint-Germain wins 1996 final, loses 1997 final.

What was the Inter-Cities Fairs Cup?

A forerunner to the UEFA Cup, the Inter-Cities Fairs Cup was an annual soccer competition held between 1955 and 1971. It was set up to promote international trade fairs in European cities and featured teams from those cities playing in matches timed to coincide with such fairs. The first Fairs Cup involved teams from Barcelona, Basle, Birmingham, Copenhagen, Frankfurt, Lausanne, Leipzig, London, Milan, and Zagreb. Barcelona beat a London 8–2 on aggregate in a two-leg final.

How was the UEFA Cup started?

The UEFA Cup grew out of the Inter-Cities Fairs Cup after the *Union des Associations Européennes de Football* took over the competition in 1971 at which time UEFA disassociated the cup from trade fairs. The competition was traditionally open to the runners-up of domestic leagues, but it was merged with UEFA's previous second-tier European competition, the UEFA Cup Winners' Cup, in 1999. Since then, the winners of domestic cup competitions have also entered the UEFA Cup.

Five Clubs That Have Received the UEFA Badge of Honour
- Real Madrid CF after six European Champion Clubs' Cup wins, 1956–60 and 1966.
- Netherlands AFC Ajax after their third consecutive European Champion Clubs' Cup win in 1973.
- FC Bayern München, after their third consecutive European Champion Clubs' Cup win in 1976.
- AC Milan, after their fifth European Champion Clubs' Cup win in 1994.
- Liverpool FC, after their fifth European Champion Clubs' Cup win in 2005.

What is the UEFA Badge of Honour?

The European Champion Clubs' Cup is a trophy awarded annually by UEFA to the football club that wins its top seasonal competition, the UEFA Champions League. After five wins or three consecutive wins, a club is entitled to keep the cup, with a new cup being forged for the next season. The UEFA Badge of Honour is awarded to such clubs and it is worn sewn to the team's shirts.

What is the UEFA Super Cup?

The UEFA Super Cup is awarded to the team that wins an annual match between the reigning champions of the UEFA Cup and the Champions League.

Why was the UEFA Intertoto Cup launched?

Originally called the International Football Cup, the UEFA Intertoto Cup was launched in 1961 by player/coach Karl Rappen, and businessman Ernst Thommen, a future FIFA vice-president who was involved in the soccer pools in Switzerland. It was conceived as a competition that would keep the business of betting active during the summer season. "Toto" in German means "pools." The UEFA Intertoto Cup was abolished after the 2008 season.

Quickies

Did you know ...
• the UEFA Cup will be renamed the UEFA Europa League in 2009–10?

Why was South Africa disqualified from the inaugural African Cup of Nations?

The Confederation of African Football (CAF) was founded on February 8, 1957, in Khartoum, Sudan, by the Football Associations of Egypt, Ethiopia, South Africa, and Sudan. The same four nations were to compete in the CAF's inaugural African Cup of Nations in Sudan later that month. But no sooner had South Africa signed on than they were disqualified, having failed to field a multiracial team due to their government's policy of apartheid. Over two games, Egypt defeated both Sudan and Ethiopia to take the cup in what might be the shortest international cup competition on record.

Who was Bernardo O'Higgins?

Bernardo O'Higgins Riquelme was one of the commanders of the military forces that freed Chile from Spanish rule in the Chilean War of Independence during the 18th century. His name was given to the Copa Bernardo O'Higgins, which was played on five occasions between 1955 and 1966 between Brazil and Chile.

Who was Carlos Padrós?

Carlos Padrós Rubio was a founding member of Real Madrid and later served as club president between 1904 and 1908. He was the driving force behind the creation of the Copa del Rey, which was first played in 1902 to celebrate the coronation of Alfonso XIII. Carlos Padrós refereed the first-ever Copa del Rey final, in which Club Vizcaya defeated FC Barcelona 2–1.

What is a *scudetto*?

Scudetto in Itlalian means "little shield," and in soccer it refers to a badge in the colours of the Italian flag, awarded annually to the championship club in the Lega Calcio Serie A, located at the top echelon of the Italian soccer league system. The winning team will wear the badge on their jersey in the following season. The first time *scudetto* were used was in 1924 when Genoa CFC won its eighth championship title. They have not won it since.

Why was there no *scudetto* champion in the *Lega Calcio Serie A* 1926–27 season?

In the 1926–27 season, title-winners Torino were stripped of their *scudetto* after an investigation by the Italian Football Federation found that a Torino official bribed opposing defender Luigi Allemandi in Torino's match against Juventus FC on June 5, 1927, and thus the season finished with no declared champions.

Six French Teams with Multiple *Trophée des Champions* Wins
- Olympique Lyonnais: 7 wins (1973, 2002, 2003, 2004, 2005, 2006, 2007)
- Stade Reims: 5 wins (1949, 1955, 1958, 1960, 1966)
- AS Saint-Étienne: 5 wins (1957, 1962, 1967, 1968, 1969)
- AS Monaco FC: 4 wins (1961, 1985, 1997, 2000)
- FC Nantes: 3 wins (1965, 1999, 2001)
- FC Girondins de Bordeaux: 2 wins (1986, 2008)
- Paris Saint-Germain FC: 2 wins (1995, 1998)

What is the *Trophée des Champions*?

Le Trophée des Champions, or the Champions Trophy, is a cup organized by the French Football Federation; a match between the winners of the French Championship and the winners of the French Cup.

What is the Triple Crown of Brazilian football?

The Triple Crown of Brazilian Football is an unofficial title given to the club that wins the three most important competitions in Brazilian soccer in the same year: the Brazilian Football State Championship, the *Copa do Brasil*, and the *Campeonato Brasileiro Série A* (Brazilian Championship First Level). Cruzeiro Esporte Clube, from the city of Belo Horizonte, is the only team to have done so (in 2003).

> **Quickies**
> *Did you know ...*
> • since 1927, the president of France has always presented the Coupe de France to the winning team's captain? Gaston Doumergue was the first to do so.

Who is the Copa Libertadores named after?

The Copa Libertadores is an annual soccer-cup competition between the top clubs of South America, and in recent editions Mexico. The name of the tournament is an homage to the "Libertadores," the main leaders of the independence wars of Latin America: Simón Bolívar, José de San Martín, Antonio José de Sucre, Bernardo O'Higgins, Ramon Castilla, and José Gervasio Artigas.

Who was Lamar Hunt?

The man who gives his name to North America's Major League Soccer (MLS) championship — the Lamar Hunt U.S. Open Cup — was a sportsman and essential promoter of soccer in the United States. He was one of the founders of MLS as well as its predecessor, the North American Soccer League (NASL). At his death in 2006 he owned two MLS teams, Columbus Crew and FC Dallas.

What is the Voyageurs Cup?

The Voyageurs Cup is the only trophy for top-level professional soccer in Canada. From 2002 to 2007, the cup was awarded annually to the Canadian United Soccer Leagues division team finishing with the best record from regular season matches against other Canadian teams in the USL. From 2008 until at least 2010, the trophy will be awarded to the winner of the Canadian Championship. Montreal Impact has won the cup every year so far.

Has Canada ever won a major international tournament?

Thrice, actually. The first time was at the 1904 Summer Olympic Games, in St. Louis. Canada sent Galt FC as their representative team and they defeated the only two other teams entered without being scored on. The second instance was more challenging as Canada competed in a field of nine national teams from the Confederation of North, Central American and Caribbean Association Football to win the 1985 CONCACAF Championship. Then in 2000 they emerged victorious from a field of eight teams to take the CONCACAF Gold Cup.

Quickies
Did you know ...
- Iraq was banned from the competition in the Arab Nations Cup from 1991 to 2002, and from the Gulf Cup of Nations from 1991 to 2003 due to the Gulf War?

What is *Khaleeji*?

Quickies
Did you know ...
- the 2013 Gulf Cup of Nations is scheduled to take place in Iraq?

Khaleeji is the Arabic name for the Gulf Cup of Nations, a tournament first held in 1970 and played every two years between Arab countries around the Persian Gulf.

What year was soccer introduced in the Olympics?

Both the 1900 and 1904 Olympic games featured men's soccer tournaments as demonstration matches, with three teams competing at each tournament. The IOC has subsequently upgraded the tournaments to official status with medals attributed to the teams based upon the match results, though FIFA does not recognize them as official. In 1908, in London, soccer was an official Olympic game with eight teams competing.

Gulf Cup of Nations century club
- March 03, 1988 — Kuwait reached 100 cumulative goals against Qatar.
- Oct. 19, 1996 — Saudi Arabia reached 100 cumulative goals against Qatar.
- Dec. 16, 2004 — Qatar reached 100 cumulative goals against Oman.

Olympic Soccer Gold-Medal Holders, Ranked by Country					
Rank	Country	Gold	Silver	Bronze	Total
1	Hungary	3	1	1	5
2	Great Britain	3	0	0	3
3	Argentina	2	2	0	4
4	Soviet Union	2	0	3	5
5	Uruguay	2	0	0	2
6	Yugoslavia	1	3	1	5
7	Poland and Spain	1	2	0	3
8	East Germany	1	1	2	4
9	Czechoslovakia, France, and Nigeria	1	1	0	2
10	Italy and Sweden	1	0	2	3
11	Belgium	1	0	1	2
12	Cameroon and Canada	1	0	0	1

What is the individual scoring record for a single player in an Olympic soccer game?

In 1908 Denmark's Sophus "Krølben" Nielsen set an Olympic record by scoring 10 goals in a 17–1 win against France. His team went on to take the silver in the final against Great Britain. Gottfried Fuchs achieved the same feat scoring 10 goals for Germany against Russia at the 1912 Olympics.

In the 1920 final, why did the Czech team walk from the field of play without finishing the match?

The 1920 Olympic games were held in Antwerp, Belgium, and saw the host nation's soccer team advanced to the final against Czechoslovakia. It was an unruly and violent game. Shortly after Czech left-back Karel Steiner was ejected in the 39th minute for a bad foul, the Czech team walked off the field in protest. They were unhappy with the performance of the 65-year-old English referee, John Lewis, as well as the English linesmen, Charles Wreford-Brown and A. Knight. They were also unnerved by the appearance of Belgian soldiers who surrounded the pitch during the match. Belgium, who led, 2–0, took the gold medal by default.

Teams With the Most Olympic Outings and No Medals

Country	Olympiads Attended	Medals Won
Egypt	10	0
Mexico	8	0
South Korea	8	0
Australia	7	0
Morroco	6	0
Turkey	5	0
Luxembourg	5	0

What year were professional players first allowed to compete in Olympic soccer?

For the 1984 Los Angeles Games, the IOC decided to admit professional players to Olympic soccer. But a conflict arose with FIFA, who did not want the Olympics to rival the World Cup. A compromise was struck that allowed teams from Africa, Asia, Oceania, and CONCACAF (the Confederation of North, Central American and Caribbean Association Football) to field their strongest professional players, while only allowing the historically stronger nations in UEFA (Union of European Football Associations) and CONMEBOL (South American Football Confederation) to pick players who had not previously played in a World Cup.

Stadiums to Be Used for Soccer in the 2012 London Olympic Games	
City	Stadium
London	Wembley Stadium
Glasgow	Hampden Park
Cardiff	Millennium Stadium
Manchester	Old Trafford
Newcastle upon Tyne	St. James' Park
Birmingham	Villa Park

Has the Olympic gold medal in soccer ever been decided in a shootout?

Only once — at the 2000 Sydney Games. On September 30, Pierre Wome of Cameroon scored the winning penalty kick as his team outscored Spain 5–3 in the shootout, after the two teams were tied 2–2 after two overtimes. The following Monday was declared a national holiday by Cameroon's president.

great players

Why was English soccer player Bobby Moore jailed in Colombia on his way to a 1970 World Cup tournament in Mexico?

Bobby Moore, the 1966 World Cup Player of the Tournament, was named England's captain for the 1970 World Cup. While in Bogotá, Colombia, where England was involved in a warm-up game, an attempt was made to implicate Moore in the theft of a bracelet from a jeweller. A young assistant had claimed that Moore had removed the bracelet from a hotel shop without paying for it. Moore was arrested and then released, but he then travelled with the England team to play another match against Ecuador in Quito. Upon his return to Mexico, Moore was detained and placed under house arrest, but diplomatic pressure, plus the weakness of the evidence, eventually saw the case dropped entirely.

Why was Italian player Luigi Allemandi once banned from football for life?

At the end of the 1926–27 season, a newspaper article prompted the Italian Football Federation to investigate misdeeds connected to a title match between Milan's Juventus team and their city rivals, Torino. The investigation discovered that defender Luigi Allemandi had accepted a 50,000-lire bribe from a Torino official to under-perform. Allemandi was supposedly banned from the game for life, but he was granted an amnesty the following year when the Italian football team won bronze at the Olympics, and he eventually took the Italian national team to victory at the 1934 World Cup as their captain.

> **Quickies**
> *Did you know ...*
> - in May 2005, in order to raise money for his family, Alan Ball sold his World Cup winner's medal and tournament cap at an auction for £140,000?

Who was the "Little Bird"?

When he was an infant, Brazilian player Manuel Francisco dos Santos suffered from severe physical disabilities: his spine was deformed, his right leg bent inwards, and his left leg was 2.4 inches (six centimetres) shorter and curved outwards. An operation that enabled him to walk left him with a distorted leg. He nonetheless grew up to become a speedy winger with the nickname *Garrincha*, which means "little bird." He won the World Cup in 1958 and 1962. He died of alcohol poisoning in 1983 at the age of 49.

Animalistic player nicknames
- Lionel Andrés Messi — Atomic Flea
- Iker Casillas — *El Gato* (The Cat)
- Claudio Lopez — *El Piojo* (The Louse)
- Gennaro Gattuso — The Pit Bull
- Eusebio — The Black Panther
- Kevin Keegan — Mighty Mouse
- Jack Charlton — The Giraffe
- Marco Van Basten — The Swan of Utrecht
- Arthur Friedenreich — The Tiger

What is the most lucrative contract ever awarded to a professional soccer player?

In January 2007 it was announced that midfielder David Beckham was leaving the Real Madrid squad to join the Los Angeles Galaxy, part of Major League Soccer (MLS), the North American men's pro league. The contract included a US$6.5-million annual salary, sponsorship deals estimated at $25 million per year, merchandise sales worth approximately $10 million per year, and a $10 million/year share of club profits. In total, the five-year contract would award him in the range of $250 million, putting him third at the time on the list of the world's highest-paid athletes, behind only Tiger Woods and Michael Schumacher.

Quickies
Did you know ...
- by the time David Beckham set foot in Los Angeles after signing his contract with their team, the Galaxy, over 250,000 Beckham jerseys had already been sold?

How many fans came out to see David Beckham's first start in a regulation MLS soccer match?

David Beckham's first start in a regulation match as a member of Major League Soccer's Los Angeles Galaxy team was played on Aug 18, 2007, against the New York Red Bulls. Held at Giants Stadium, in East Rutherford, New Jersey, the game drew a crowd of 66,237 fans, up considerably from the Red Bulls' average draw of 11,573 fans. The Red Bulls won 5–4.

Professional Soccer's Highest-Earning Players for 2008		
Player	Club	Approximate Income (USD)
David Beckham	Los Angeles Galaxy	$37 million
Ronaldinho	Barcelona	$29 million
Lionel Andrés Messi	Barcelona	$27 million
Cristiano Ronaldo	Manchester United	$23 million
Thierry Henry	Barcelona	$20 million
John Terry	Chelsea	$16.5 million
Michael Ballack	Chelsea	$16.5 million
Ronaldo	AC Milan	$16 million
Kaká	AC Milan	$15.3 million
Steven Gerrard	Liverpool	$14 million

What is the "Beckham Rule"?

When David Beckham joined the Los Angeles Galaxy in 2007, his deal fell under special league rule called the "Designated Player Rule." The rule allows each MLS franchise to sign one player that would be considered outside of the team's salary cap, allowing American and Canadian

Quickies
Did you know ...
- within six months after David Beckham joined with Real Madrid in 2003, the team had sold over one million replica Beckham jerseys?

teams to compete for star players in the international soccer market. Only US$400,000 of the Designated Player's contract is held against the franchise's salary cap. David Beckham was the first player signed (by the Los Angeles Galaxy) under this rule and thus it was dubbed the "Beckham Rule."

Current Designated Players of the MLS		
Player	Team	Salary (USD)
Juan Pablo Ángel	New York Red Bulls	$1,593,750
David Beckham	Los Angeles Galaxy	$6,500,004
Cuauhtémoc Blanco	Chicago Fire	$2,666,778
Luciano Emilio	D.C. United	$758,857
Marcelo Gallardo	D.C. United	$1,874,006
Freddie Ljungberg	Seattle Sounders FC	$2,500,000
Claudio López	Kansas City Wizards	$820,000
Guillermo Barros Schelotto	Columbus Crew	$375,000

Why did spies kill Lutz Eigendorf?

On March 20, 1979, after a friendly match between the East German team Berliner FC Dynamo and West German club 1. FC Kaiserslautern, East German midfielder Lutz Eigendorf defected to the West. It might not have been the wisest move, given that FC Dynamo was under the patronage of the Stasi, East Germany's secret police. After German reunification in 1990 and the subsequent opening of Stasi files it was revealed that the traffic accident on March 5, 1983, that led to Eigendorf's death two days later had been staged as an assassination by the Stasi.

Who was A.H. Chequer?

A.H. Chequer was the pseudonym under which star English sportsman Morton Betts played during the 1872 FA Cup final. Betts played under the false name because he was "cup-tied," meaning he was technically ineligible to play in the match after having transferred from another club in the same competition. Betts had begun the tournament registered with Harrow Chequers FC, but they had withdrawn prior to the first game. Betts became the first player to ever score in an FA Cup final, giving The Wanderers a 1–0 victory over the Royal Engineers.

Quickies
Did you know ...
• Matthias Sammer scored the last ever goal for the East Germany football team before German reunification?

Who is Edson Arantes Do Nascimento?

Edson Arantes Do Nascimento is better known by his nickname: Pelé. The Brazilian former footballer, rated by many as the greatest of all time, was given the title of Athlete of the Century by the International Olympic Committee in 1999. He remains the all-time top scorer in the history of the Brazil national soccer team and is the only footballer to be a part of three World Cup–winning teams, with Brazil in 1958, 1962, and 1970.

Archetype Player Nicknames
• Mario Kempes — *El Matador* (The Bullfighter)
• Paul Scholes — Ginger Ninja
• Eidur Gudjohnsen — Ice Man
• Pablo Aimar — *El Payaso* (The Clown)
• Javier Zanetti — The Tractor
• Julio Baptista — The Beast

What does "Pelé" mean?

The name "Pelé" has no meaning in Portuguese, the language of Pelé's homeland, Brazil. The nickname was given to him as a taunt by a schoolmate when Pelé was young. In Hebrew, it means

Quickies
Did you know ...
• when a schoolmate of Pelé's came up with his nickname, Pelé punched the boy and received a two-day suspension?

"miracle." It is also the name of a Hawaiian volcano goddess. It also resembles the Irish language word *peile*, meaning football.

Has any player ever won the World Cup as a player and later as a coach?

Regarded by many as the greatest German footballer of all time, sweeper Franz Beckenbauer won the 1974 World Cup as a player, and the 1990 World Cup as a coach, both times with West Germany.

What is the largest number of goals scored by a player in a single match?

It's a tie. In December 1942, Stephan Stanis of Racing Club de Lens scored 16 goals in a French Cup match against Aubry Asturies. In May 2007, Olympos Xylofagou FC saw their striker Panagiotis Pontikos score 16 goals against SEK Ayios Athanasios FC.

Who was Alexander Morten?

Alexander Morten was England's goalkeeper and captain when they beat Scotland 4–2 in England's second official international match, held at the Kennington

Oval on March 8, 1873. Interestingly, Morten had already appeared in an international between the two countries, but as Scotland's goalkeeper in the first unofficial international between the two counties, which was held Kennington Oval on March 5, 1870, and ended in a 1–1 draw.

Who was the first Chinese player to appear for England?

Frank Soo was the first player of Chinese extraction to play for England. He was born in Buxton, Derbyshire, in 1914 and was the son of a Chinese father and an English mother. One of the best inside forwards of the immediate pre-war era, he formed part of a legendary team that included players such as Sir Stanley Matthews and Neil Franklin.

Who holds the record for most goals in a career?

Josef "Pepi" Bican was a Czech-Austrian football forward. Records are not entirely complete, but it has been estimated by soccer statisticians that Bican scored 800 goals in all of his competitive matches, not including friendly games. For this, the International Federation of Football Historians and Statisticians awarded Bican the "Golden Ball" as the greatest goal-scorer of the last century.

Sudden Death 1

Players (by name and team) who died of heart attacks during or shortly following soccer matches or training:

Ivan Karacić (NK Široki Brijeg), Antonio Puerta (Sevilla FC), Chase Nsofwa (Hapoel Beersheba), Mohamed Abdelwahab (Ahly), Matt Gadsby (Hinckley United), Alin Paicu (Minerul Matasari), Suad Katana (Lokeren), Nedžad Botonjc (Ljubljana), Paul Sykes (Folkestone Invicta), Hugo Cunha (Uniao Leiria), Bruno Baião (SL Benfica), Serginho (São Caetano), Andrej Pawitskij (Arsenal Kiev), Danny Ortiz (CSD Municipal), Miklós Fehér (SL Benfica), Marc-Vivien Foé (Cameroon), Landu Ndonbasi (Oliveira de Frades), Catalin Hîldan (Dinamo Bucharest), Eri Irianto (Persebaya Surabaya), Stefan Vrabioru (SC Astra Ploiesti), Robbie James (Llanelli), Axel Jüptner (FC Carl Zeiss Jena), Markus Paßlack (Fortuna Dusseldorf), Emmanuel Nwanegbo (SSV Reutlingen), Waheeb Jabarra (Hapoel Taibe), Amir Angwe (Julius Berger FC), Michael Klein (Bayer Uerdingen), David Longhurst (York City), Samuel Okwaraji (Nigeria), Paulo Navalho (Atlético Clube de Portugal), Omar Sahnoun (Girondins de Bordeaux), Renato Curi (Perugia), Michel Soulier (Union Royale Namur), Pavão (FC Porto), Giuliano Taccola (A.S. Roma).

Who was the first non-English manager to lead a team to the FA Cup Championship?

As a player, Ruud Gullit was captain of Holland when they took the 1988 European Championship. He went on to net two consecutive European Cups and three Italian league titles with AC Milan. After retiring from play, he became manager of Chelsea FC in 1996. The next year he became the first non-Englishman to claim a major trophy with Chelsea's 1997 FA Cup win over Middlesbrough.

Quickies

Did you know ...

- the record for most World Cup matches played belongs to Lothar Matthaus of Germany, who played 25 World Cup games in his career?

What is the FIFA World Player of the Year award?

The FIFA World Player of the Year is an Association Football award given annually to the player thought to be the best in the world, based on votes by coaches and captains of international teams.

What is the Ballon d'Or?

Conceived in 1956 by *France Football* magazine's chief writer Gabriel Hanot, the Ballon d'Or, often referred to as the European Footballer of the Year award, is an annual association football award decided by sports journalists. It is presented to the player considered to have performed the best over the previous calendar year. Originally, only players of European nationality were eligible. In 1995 the field was expanded to include non-Europeans who played with European clubs. In 2007, the competition was opened to all Association Football players around the world. The trophy is a golden soccer ball, hence the name of the award.

Why was Iraqi defender Barmeer Shaker given a one-year suspension by FIFA?

On June 8, 1986, during a first-round World Cup match against Belgium, Iraqi defender Barmeer Shaker spat at the referee. He was subsequently suspended for one year by FIFA and

Quickies
Did you know ...
- on June 11, 1986, Paraguayan coach Cayetano Re became the first coach to be sent off in World Cup finals, for standing too close to the field?

FIFA World Player of the Year Winners

2008	Cristiano Ronaldo (Portugal)
2007	Kaká (Brazil)
2006	Fabio Cannavaro (Italy)
2005	Ronaldinho (Brazil)
2004	Ronaldinho (Brazil)
2003	Zinedine Zidane (France)
2002	Ronaldo (Brazil)
2001	Luis Figo (Portugal)
2000	Zinedine Zidane (France)
1999	Rivaldo (Brazil)
1998	Zinedine Zidane (France)
1997	Ronaldo (Brazil)
1996	Ronaldo (Brazil)
1995	George Weah (Liberia)
1994	Romário (Brazil)
1993	Roberto Baggio (Italy)
1992	Marco van Basten (Netherlands)
1991	Lothar Matthäus (Germany)

Players With Multiple Ballon d'Or Wins

Name	Country		Years
Johan	Netherlands	3	1971, 1973, 1974
Michel	France	3	1983, 1984, 1985
Marco van Basten	Netherlands	3	1988, 1989, 1992
Alfredo di Stéfano	Spain	2	1957, 1959
Franz Beckenbauer	Germany	2	1972, 1976
Kevin Keegan	England	2	1978, 1979
Karl-Heinz Rummenigge	Germany	2	1980, 1981
Ronaldo	Brazil	2	1997, 2002

Players With All-Time Double-Digit World Cup Scoring Records

Ronaldo (Brazil)	15
Gerd Müller (Germany)	14
Juste Fontaine (France)	13
Pelé (Brazil)	12
Sandor Kocsis (Hungary)	11
Jürgen Klinsmann (Germany)	11
Helmut Rahn (Germany)	10
Teofilo Cubillas (Peru)	10
Gary Lineker (England)	10
Grzegorz Lato (Poland)	10
Gabriel Batistuta (Argentina)	10
Miroslav Klose (Germany)	10

Iraq lost the match to Belgium 2–1. It was the first and only time that Iraq has qualified for the World Cup.

What player holds the record for most European Championship goals in a single tournament?

Michel Platini holds the record for European Championship goals after captaining France to the 1984 title on home soil and finding the net nine times during the competition. Platini represented France a total of 72 times, with a record 41 goals for his country.

Who is called the "White Pelé"?

Before he retired from play in 1994, Artur Antunes Coimbra — better known as Zico — scored 66 goals in 88 international matches for Brazil, and represented them in the 1978, 1982, and 1986 World Cups. Often called the White Pelé, he is commonly considered one of the most skilled dribblers ever and was a master of the free kick. In 2003, Pelé said, "Throughout the years, the one player that came closest to me was Zico." Zico is also one of the best players in football history not to have been on a World Cup–winning squad.

Why are there 125 players on the FIFA 100 list?

The FIFA 100 is Pelé's list of the "greatest living footballers." He chose 125 players to be on the list, which seems incongruous with the list's name until you understand that the list was unveiled on March 4, 2004, at a gala ceremony in London, marking part of the celebrations of the 100th anniversary of the *Fédération Internationale de Football Association* (FIFA). The "100" of the list name refers to the anniversary, not the number of players Pelé chose.

Who was "The Great Dane"?

Peter Schmeichel has been called the greatest goaltender to have ever played the game. Nicknamed "The Great Dane," he was born in Gladsaxe, Denmark, and played in his home nation until 1992, when the Danish team took the UEFA European Championship. He then joined Manchester United and was captain of their 1999 squad that won an unprecedented Treble (to win a country's top division and two cup competitions in the same season), taking the English Premiership, FA Cup, and UEFA Champions League all in the same season.

Man United's Record With Peter Schmeichel Between the Posts

• Premier League: 1992–93, 1993–94, 1995–96, 1996–97, 1998–99
• FA Cup: 1994, 1996, 1999
• FA Charity Shield: 1993, 1994, 1996, 1997
• Football League Cup: 1992
• European Super Cup: 1991
• UEFA Champions League: 1998–99

Who was Alfie Conn Jr.?

Midfielder Alfie Conn Jr. was not only the first player to compete for both Rangers and Celtic in the postwar period, in 1977 he became the first player to win the Scottish Cup finals with both Old Firm teams. In 1973, on May 3, he scored the second goal in a 3–2 final victory over Celtic at Hampden Park. In 1977, although he didn't score in the match, he won another Scottish Cup medal with Celtic when they defeated Rangers 1–0 in the final at Hampden on May 7.

Why was Hungarian player Ferenc Puskás called "The Galloping Major"?

In 1949 Soviet-controlled Hungary, Ferenc Puskás was playing for Kispest AC near Budapest. That year, the Kispest club was taken over by the Hungarian Ministry of Defence, becoming the Hungarian Army team and changing its name to Honvéd. All players were given military ranks. Puskás became a major, which eventually led to the nickname "The Galloping Major." Puskás later defected to play for Real Madrid, winning five Spanish titles. In 1993, the Hungarian government granted him a full pardon, allowing him to return and take charge of the national team.

Quickies

Did you know ...

- in his debut professional season, playing for Brazilian club Cruzeiro in 1993, future superstar Ronaldo scored 58 goals in 60 matches?

Who was Henri Delaunay?

Henri Delaunay was a French soccer player, referee, and administrator. In 1927, he was the first person to propose a pan-European tournament.

Players Noted For Their Noticeable Locks	
Player	Worst Hairstyle
Christian Wilhelmsson	Cockatiel faux-hawk mullet
Ronaldo	The forehead wedge
Roberto Baggio	Businessman with a ponytail
Taribo West	Green cornrows
Sir Bobby Charlton	The comb-over
Carlos Valderrama	Frizzy plug-socket afro
Alexi Lalas	Billy-goatee
Rodrigo Palacio	Rat-tail braid
Djibril Cisse	Peroxide gone wrong
David Beckham	You name it, he's done it

When just such a tournament — the quadrennial UEFA European Football Championship — was launched in 1958, its trophy was named after the visionary.

What peculiar thing did Brazillian player Leonidas do in a 1938 World Cup match against Poland?

On June 5, in Strasbourg, at the start of a 1938 World Cup first-round match against Poland, star Brazilian player Leonidas took off his soccer boots because he wanted to play in the muddy pitch barefooted. He scored three goals in the match, including two in extra time, to help Brazil advance to the quarter-finals.

What embarrassed Italian player Peppino Meazza during the 1938 World Cup semifinal?

As Meazza scored on a penalty kick, his shorts, torn earlier in the game, fell down. His celebrating teammates surrounded him until a new pair were produced. Italy went on to win the game, and the tournament.

Sudden Death 2
Players (by name and team) who died of head trauma during or shortly following soccer matches or training:
Sim Raleigh, (Gillingham), Horace Fairhurst (Blackpool), Thomas Blackstock (Manchester United), Tunde Charity (Bendel Insurance), Ferenc Biro (Nirajul Miercurea-Nir), Gabriel Talpoş (Minerul Rodna), Hocine Gacemi (JS Kabylie), Serhiy Perkhun (CSKA Moscow), Hrvoje Ćustić (NK Zadar).

How did Wolfgang Weber silence Wembley stadium in 1966?

In the 1966 World Cup final in London's Wembley Stadium, England faced off against West Germany. As regulation time drew to a close, England was up 2–1. But then in the 89th minute, German player Wolfgang Weber silenced the Wembley crowd by scoring. The game had to be decided in extra time, with England eventually taking the championship 4–1, on goals from Geoff Hurst at the 101-minute and 120-minute marks. Those two goals completed a hat trick for Hurst in the match.

Quickies
Did you know ...
• Hungarian forward Ferenc Puskás scored 84 goals in 85 international matches for Hungary?

Who holds the record for longest professional playing career?

Sir Stanley Matthews, the only English player to have been knighted before retirement, was born in 1915 and started his soccer career in 1932, playing for Stoke City FC at the age of 17. He stayed with them until 1947, then moved to Blackpool FC until 1961, at which point he returned to Stoke City FC He played his final game with Stoke on February 6, 1965, just after his 50th birthday, achieving the record of longest professional career at 33 years. Considered to have been one of the greatest players ever, Matthews died in February 2000.

Who were the Bubsy Babes?

Recruited and trained in the 1950s, the Busby Babes were a group of young Manchester United players who progressed from the club's youth team into the first team under coach Matt Busby. The nickname for the group, said to have been coined by *Manchester Evening News* journalist Tom Jackson, refers to the players who won the league championship in seasons 1955–56 and 1956–57 with an average age of 21 and 22 respectively. In 1958, eight of the Busby Babes were killed while returning from a European Cup match in Belgrade. After making a refuelling stop, the airplane they were in crashed while trying to take off from a slushy Munich airfield.

Munich Air Disaster of 1958	
Fatalities	Survivors
Geoff Bent	Johnny Berry
Roger Byrne	Jackie Blanchflower
Eddie Colman	Bobby Charlton
Duncan Edwards (survived, but died in hospital 15 days later)	Bill Foulkes
Mark Jones	Harry Gregg
David Pegg	Kenny Morgans
Tommy Taylor	Albert Scanlon
Liam "Billy" Whelan	Dennis Viollet
Walter Crickmer (club secretary)	Ray Wood
Tom Curry (trainer)	Matt Busby (manager)
Bert Whalley (chief coach)	

Has anyone scored a hat trick in an FA Cup final?

Appropriately enough, three people have done so. Billy Townley did it for Blackburn Rovers in 1890, Jimmy Logan did it for Notts County in 1894, and Stan Mortensen scored three for Blackpool in 1953. No one has done it since.

Who are UEFA's Golden Players?

To celebrate the Union of European Football Associations (UEFA)'s 50th anniversary in 2004, each of its member associations was asked by UEFA to choose one of its own players as the single most outstanding player of the previous 50 years (1954–2003). The 52 players were known as the "UEFA Golden Players."

The 52 UEFA Golden Players

Albania — Panajot Pano
Andorra — Koldo
Armenia — Khoren Hovhannisyan
Austria — Herbert Prohaska
Azerbaijan — Anatoliy Banishevskiy
Belarus — Sergei Aleinikov
Belgium — Paul Van Himst
Bosnia and Herzegovina — Safet Sušić
Bulgaria — Hristo Stoichkov
Croatia — Davor Šuker
Cyprus — Sotiris Kaiafas
Czech Republic — Josef Masopust
Denmark — Michael Laudrup
England — Bobby Moore
Estonia — Mart Poom
Faroe Islands — Abraham Løkin
Finland — Jari Litmanen
France — Just Fontaine
Georgia — Murtaz Khurtsilava
Germany — Fritz Walter
Greece — Vassilis Hatzipanagis
Hungary — Ferenc Puskás
Iceland — Ásgeir Sigurvinsson
Republic of Ireland — Johnny Giles
Israel — Mordechai Spiegler
Italy — Dino Zoff

Kazakhstan — Sergey Kvochkin
Latvia — Aleksandrs Starkovs
Liechtenstein — Rainer Hasler
Lithuania — Arminas Narbekovas
Luxembourg — Louis Pilot
Macedonia — Darko Pancev
Malta — Carmel Busuttil
Moldova — Pavel Cebanu
Netherlands — Johan Cruyff
Northern Ireland — George Best
Norway — Rune Bratseth
Poland — Włodzimierz Lubański
Portugal — Eusébio
Romania — Gheorghe Hagi
Russia — Lev Yashin
San Marino — Massimo Bonini
Scotland — Denis Law
Serbia and Montenegro — Dragan Džajić
Slovakia — Ján Popluhár
Slovenia — Branko Oblak
Spain — Alfredo Di Stéfano
Sweden — Henrik Larsson
Switzerland — Stéphane Chapuisat
Turkey — Hakan Sükür
Ukraine — Oleg Blokhin
Wales — John Charles

Who was the first winner of the "Golden Boot"?

The European Golden Boot, which is now actually known as The European Golden Shoe, is an award presented each season by European soccer journalists to the leading goal-scorer in league matches from the top division of every European national league. The first-ever recipient of the award was the Mozambique-born Portuguese player Eusebio da Silva Ferreira, who netted 42 goals in the 1967–68 season playing for S.L Benfica in Lisbon.

Who scored the first goal in FA Cup competition history?

The first official FA Cup competition goal was scored by Jarvis Kenrick for Clapham Rovers in a 3–0 victory over Upton Park on November 11, 1871. It was the first of two goals for Kenrick in the match. He later won the FA Cup three years running with Wanderers.

Who discovered Johan Cruijff?

When he was a boy, Dutch superstar player Johan Cruijff's mother worked as a cleaner at the AFC Ajax grounds in Amsterdam and it was she who persuaded the Ajax coaches to admit her son to their youth development system at the age of 12, in 1959. She was a good scout. As one of the greatest players ever to emerge from the Netherlands, Cruijff would eventually help Ajax win eight Eredivisie league championships and seven KNVB Cups.

Sudden Death 3		
Players Killed by Lightning Strikes on the Pitch		
Date	Player	Team
October 24, 2002	Hernán Gaviria	Deportivo Cali
October 24, 2002	Giovanni Córdoba	Deportivo Cali
September 32, 1984	Erik Jongbloed	DWS Amsterdam
April 12, 1979	Mohamed Ali Akid	Club Sportif Sfaxien
February 25, 1967	Tony Allden	Highgate United FC

What was the "Hand of God"?

The "Hand of God" was the hand of Argentine player Diego Maradona — his left hand to be precise. In the quarter-finals of the 1986 World Cup,

as Argentina faced England, Maradona scored in the 51st minute on what appeared — at least to referee Ali Bennaceur — to be a header. However, virtually everyone else in attendance knew, or at least suspected, that, as Maradona and England goalkeeper Peter Shilton jumped for a ball

that was coming down into the goal area off a high kick, Maradona had punched the ball in with his raised left hand. At the post-game press conference, Maradona claimed that the goal was scored *"un poco con la cabeza de Maradona y otro poco con la mano de Dios"* ("a little with the head of Maradona and a little with the hand of God"). It turned out it was *a lot* with the hand of Maradona, as press photos appeared over the ensuing days clearly showing him punching the ball. Argentina defeated England 2–1 and went on to win the tournament. Maradona later admitted to TV that he'd hit the goal in with his hand.

Which club brought Brazilian superstar Romario to Europe?

Brazilian striker Ramario began his senior career in 1985 with C.R. Vasco da Gama in Rio de Janeiro and played for them until 1888 when he rose to international

recognition as the top scorer at the Olympic football tournament in South Korea. That year, PSV Eindhoven in the Netherlands brought him to Europe, and in exchange he helped them win the Dutch League championship in 1989, 1991, and 1992, as well as the KNVB Cup in 1989 and 1990.

Who was the first player sent off in a League Cup final?

Andrei Kanchelskis became the first player to be sent off in a League Cup final when he was shown the red card for Manchester United against Aston Villa in 1994?

What is the George Best Egg?

George Best, who died of illness related to alcoholism on October 3, 2005, was one of the greatest players ever to have come out of Northern Ireland. In June 2006, Sarah Fabergé — great-granddaughter of Russian Imperial Jeweller Carl Fabergé — was commissioned to create the George Best Egg as a tribute. A limited edition of 68 eggs — which feature the figure of a soccer player inside — were produced, with all profits from the sale of the eggs going to the George Best Foundation, which raises money for local football and research into liver disease and alcoholism. The first egg from the collection is now on permanent public display at the Belfast Airport, which was renamed the George Best Airport in May 2006.

> **Quickies**
> *Did you know ...*
> • just before his 14th birthday, Thierry Henry was one of only 25 boys that year selected to attend the French Football Federation's prestigious Clairefontaine Academy outside of Paris?

Why did French captain Zinedine Zidane head-butt Italian player Marco Materazzi during extra time in the 2006 World Cup final?

In one of the most infamous moments in modern international soccer, French player Zinedine Zidane ended his international career and destroyed any hopes his team might have had to win the 2006 World Cup by head-butting Italian player

> **Quickies**
> *Did you know ...*
> • for the first anniversary of George Best's death, Ulster Bank issued one million commemorative five-pound notes?

One-Name Player Nicknames
- Zinedine Zidane — Zizou
- Thierry Henry — Titi
- Edson Arantes Do Nascimento — Pelé
- Arthur Antunes Coimbra — Zico
- Joseph Bican — Pepi

Marco Materazzi in the chest at the 1:10 minute mark of the tournament final. The attack saw Materazzi crumple to the ground in agony and garnered Zidane a red card. Materazzi later said that after he had grabbed Zidane's jersey, Zidane offered it to him sarcastically. Materazzi then replied, "I prefer the whore that is your sister," which resulted in the head-butt. Italy went on to win the match 5–3 in a shootout. Zidane retired from professional play after the incident.

the women's game

What was the Munitionettes' Cup?

In August 1917 a tournament was held for female munitions workers' teams in northeast England. Its official title was the "Tyne Wear & Tees Alfred Wood Munitions Girls Cup," but it was popularly known as "The Munitionettes' Cup." The first winners of the trophy were Blyth Spartans, who defeated Bolckow, Vaughan 5–0 in a replayed final tie at Middlesbrough on May 18, 1918. The tournament ran for a second year in the 1918–19 season, the winners being the ladies of Palmer's shipyard in Jarrow, who defeated Christopher Brown's of Hartlepool 1–0 at St. James's Park in Newcastle on March 22, 1919.

When was women's soccer introduced into the Olympics?

Sadly, it was only in 1996 that women's soccer became an official Olympic sport.

Why haven't England, Scotland, Wales, and Northern Ireland fielded women's Olympic Soccer teams?

England and the other three British Home Nations are not eligible to compete as separate entities in women's Olympic soccer because the International Olympic Committee does not recognize their FIFA status as separate nations. As a result, Great Britain has not yet fielded a team.

Quickies

Did you know ...

- because it competed for attention with the men's game, England's FA banned women's soccer teams in 1921?

Who were the Dick, Kerr Ladies?

The Dick, Kerr Ladies was the most famous early women's football team. Founded in Preston, Lancashire, England, during the First World War, it was a works' team for the munitions manufacturer Dick, Kerr & Co., owned by W.B. Dick and John Kerr. They played friendly matches with other women's teams during the war to raise money for charity.

When was the first women's international match?

The first women's international was held in 1920 when the Dick, Kerr Ladies hosted a team from Paris for four games in England, at Deepdale, Stockport, Manchester, and London. Afterwards, the British team followed their opponents back to France and toured four French citys — Paris, Roubaix, Havre, and Rouen — to complete the tournament.

Results of the First Women's International	
Location	Results
Deepdale	England 2, France 0
Stockport	England 5, France 2
Manchester	England 1, France 1
London	England 1, France 2
Paris	England 1, France 1
Roubaix	England 2, France 0
Havre	England 6, France 0
Rouen	England 2,France 0

What was the English Ladies' Football Association?

In reaction to the FA's banning of women's football, the English Ladies' Football Association (ELFA) was formed. The first meeting of the ELFA took place at Blackburn on December 10, 1921. At that time there were approximately 150 women's football clubs in England. The representatives of 25 clubs attended the initial meeting. Sixty attended the second, held in Grimsby. ELFA existed for about two years, and held one challenge cup tournament with 24 teams entered in competition. The winners were Stoke Ladies, who defeated Doncaster and Bentley Ladies 3–1, on June 24, 1922.

Quickies
Did you know ...
• England's FA did not recognize women's soccer until 1971?

Who is Ann Kristin Aarønes?

Ann Kristin "Anka" Aarønes is a retired Norwegian soccer player. She first played for Spjelkavik IL, then for Trondheims-Ørn, and the Norwegian national team. Later she played for the WUSA's New York Power, during the first season. She was top scorer at the 1995 FIFA Women's World Cup.

Who is Linda Medalen?

One of Norway's most celebrated women footballers, Linda Medalen finished her international career with 152 caps, scoring 64 goals. She was on the Norwegian team that won the 1995 FIFA Women's World Cup.

Who is Delma Gonçalves?

Born May 19, 1975, in Rio de Janeiro, Delma Gonçalves is a Brazilian women's soccer player who currently plays as a striker for Japan's INAC Leonessa. She has been a long-time member of the Brazilian National Team for which she debuted in 1991. Her nickname is *Pretinha* ("little black girl").

Who is Birgit Prinz?

Birgit Prinz is a German soccer player and the Women's World Cup all-time leading scorer with 14 goals. Born in Frankfurt am Main, Prinz has been with 1FFC Frankfurt since July 1994. She was elected FIFA Women's World Player of the Year in 2003, 2004, and 2005 and was named German "Women's Footballer of the Year" each year from 2001 to 2007.

Quickies
Did you know ...
• in 2003, Prinz received an offer to play for AC Perugia, in Italy, and could have been the first woman to play in a professional men's league, but declined the offer?

Who is Sun Wen?

Sun Wen is a retired Chinese soccer player from Shanghai. She won both the Golden Boot and the Golden Ball for the 1999 Women's World Cup, and she became the first woman to be nominated for the Asian Football Confederation player of the year award. In 2002, she was voted FIFA's Woman Player of the Century, an award she shared with American Michelle Akers.

What was the UEFA European Competition for Representative Women's Teams?

In 1984 UEFA launched its first sanctioned international women's tournament. It was played in 1984, 1987, and 1989 under the somewhat cumbersome name of the UEFA European Competition for Representative Women's Teams. For 1991 the tournament was renamed the UEFA European Women's Championship and it is now commonly known as The Women's Euro. It has also been held in 1993, 1995, 1997, 2001, and 2005, seeing teams from England, Sweden, Finland, Denmark, Germany, France, Norway, and Italy compete.

Wins by Country for the Women's Euro	
Country	Wins
Germany	5 (1989, 1995, 1997, 2001, 2005)
Norway	2 (1987, 1993)
Sweden	1 (1984)

When was the first Women's World Cup?

The first Women's World Cup was held in China from November 16–30, 1991. The American team, led by a dominating forward line dubbed "The Triple-Edged Sword" by the Chinese media, cut through the tournament to win the first-ever world championship for women's soccer. The final, in which the United States defeated Norway 2–1, was played in front of 65,000 fans at Guangzhou's Tianhe Stadium.

Wins by Country for the Women's World Cup

Country	Wins
Germany	2
United States	2
Norway	1

Which player has appeared in the most Women's World Cups?

At the 2007 World Cup in China, U.S. captain Kristine Lilly competed in her fifth World Cup, making her the only woman — and one of three players in history — to have appeared in five World Cups.

How did Brandi Chastain celebrate a goal at the Women's World Cup?

Too be fair, it wasn't just any goal. Indeed, it was the tournament-clinching penalty kick against Norway in the 1991 Women's World Cup, and after it went into the net, Chastain came out of her shirt, tearing off her jersey and waving it in the air overhead as she fell to her knees cheering. Thankfully, she was wearing a black sports bra underneath.

Who holds the international scoring record for women's soccer?

Mia Hamm is considered by many to be the greatest woman to have ever played soccer. In 275 appearances with the American national team, she logged a record 158 goals.

Mia Hamm Championships		
Year	Team	Championship/Medal
1989	UNC	NCAA National Champion
1990	UNC	NCAA National Champion
1991	U.S. Women's National Team	FIFA World Cup Champion
1992	UNC	NCAA National Champion
1993	UNC	NCAA National Champion
1995	U.S. Women's National Team	FIFA World Cup Third Place
1996	U.S. Women's National team	Olympic Gold
1999	U.S. Women's National Team	FIFA World Cup Champion
2000	U.S. Women's National Team	Olympic Silver
2003	Washington Freedom	WUSA Founder's Cup Champion
2003	U.S. women's national team	FIFA World Cup Third Place
2004	U.S. women's national team	Olympic Gold

Why did Arsenal striker Julie Fleeting sit out the 2008–09 season?

Julie Fleeting, a Scottish international, plays for Arsenal Ladies in the Women's English Premier League. She had to inform her team that she'd be sitting out for 2008–09 because she learned in December 2008 that she was expecting a child. In June 2008 she was made an MBE by Queen Elizabeth.

Quickies
Did you know ...
• Mia Hamm is married to Major League Baseball multiple all-star Nomar Garciaparra?

Who is Marta?

Like so many other great Brazilian players, Marta Vieira Da Silva needs only one name. To Brazilians, she is simply Marta, one of the best women soccer players ever. Thrice voted FIFA World Player of the year (2006,

2007, 2008) she was a member of the Brazilian National Teams that won the silver at the Olympics in 2004 and 2008. In the 2007 Women's World Cup, she won both the Golden Ball award as the best player and the Golden Boot award as the top scorer.

Why did Maribel Dominguez's childhood friends call her Mario?

Growing up in Mexico city, Maribel Dominguez was surrounded by streets filled with boys playing soccer. Wanting to join in, she pretended to be a boy herself. She had the thin physique to pass, and kept her hair short. It wasn't until her friends saw in the newspaper that their chum "Mario" had made it onto the Mexican sub-national women's team that the penny dropped. She went on to eventually captain the senior Mexican women's team and was top goal-scorer for them at the 2004 Olympics.

Quickies

Did you know ...

- in 2004, Maribel Dominguez accepted a two-year contract from the second-division Mexican football club Celaya, but the deal was stifled by FIFA because it's a men's team?

Who was the first player sent off in Women's World Cup history?

Just six minutes into a group match against Nigeria on November 21, 1991, at Jiangmen Stadium, Chinese Taipei player Hui Fang Lin became the first ever player to be sent off in a Women's World Cup match.

Quickies

Did you know ...

- Shannon Boxx, who won a Gold at the 2004 and 2008 Olympics with the American Women's soccer team, is the younger sister of Gillian Boxx, who won the gold at the 1996 Olympics with the American softball team?

Does Michele Ackers still play soccer?

No, she's moved on to nobler endeavours. Seriously. Ackers was one of the all-time great American women soccer players, helping the American team take gold at the 1996 Olympics. But she retired from the game in 2000 and now runs a horse rescue farm in Florida.

What is the WPS?

The Women's Professional Soccer (WPS) is a top-level professional women's soccer league in the United States that launched in Spring 2009. The league replaces the Women's United Soccer Association (WUSA), which folded after its 2003 season. WPS has teams in Santa Clara (CA), Boston, Chicago, Los Angeles, New Jersey/New York, St. Louis, and Washington D.C.

Who is called Sissi?

Here is another one-name Brazillian soccer star. Sisleide do Amor Lima is best known by her nickname, Sissi. Now retired, she was a star member of the Brazil women's national football team. She won the golden boot award in the 1999 Women's World Cup in which she scored seven goals, sharing the award with China's Sun Wen. A veteran of three World Cup finals and two Olympic campaigns, she was pegged in 2008 as the new assistant coach FC Gold Pride, a professional soccer club based in Santa Clara, California, that will begin play in 2009 in the inaugural season of Women's Professional Soccer (WPS).

What two records did Kara Lang set at just 15 years old?

Canadian Kara Lang holds the women's football world record for youngest player to score a full international goal. She scored against Wales at the Algarve Cup on March 3, 2002, at age 15 years, 132 days. She must have been on a roll, because her senior debut, two days earlier, had been a Canadian record for youngest senior women's cap.

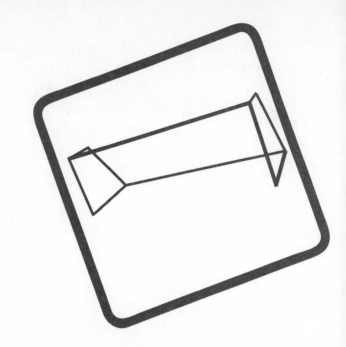

clubs and sides

What does "real" mean in Real Madrid?

Founded in 1902 Real Madrid was originally called the Madrid Football Club, or Madrid FC. In 1920, the club's name was changed to Real Madrid after King Alfonso XIII granted the team Royal patronage. "Real" means "royal."

What was the *Ye-yé* team?

Real Madrid won the European Cup for a sixth time in 1966 defeating FK Partizan 2–1 in the final with a team composed entirely of nationally born players known as the *Ye-yé* team. The name *Ye-yé* came from the "yeah, yeah, yeah" chorus in the Beatles song "She Loves You" after four members of the team posed for the *Diario Marca* sports newspaper dressed in Beatles wigs. The *Ye-yé* generation was also European Cup runner-up in 1962 and 1964.

> **Quickies**
> *Did you know ...*
> • the selection of the first president of Valencia FC, Octavio Augusto Milego, was decided by a coin toss in a bar?

Who were *La Quinta del Buitre*?

Buitre in Spanish means "Vulture." *La Quinta del Buitre* ("Vulture's Cohort"), was a group of five players on the Real Madrid squad in the 1980s. Their name, assigned by Spanish sport journalist Julio César Iglesias, was derived from the nickname given to one of its members, striker Emilio Butragueño. The other four members were Manuel Sanchís, Martín Vázquez, Míchel, and Miguel Pardeza.

Why does Valencia FC have a bat on their crest?

Valencia and the Balearic Islands were conquered by King James I of Aragon during the first half of the thirteenth century. In that period, the sight of a bat was considered to be an omen of good luck. On October 9, 1238, when James I was about to enter the city of Valencia, re-conquering it from the Moors, it is said that a bat landed on the top of his flag. He interpreted it as a good sign. When he conquered the city, the bat was added to its coat of arms. Valencia FC has adopted it for their crest.

What is *El Clásico*?

El Clásico is any football match between rivals Real Madrid and FC Barcelona. The rivalry comes about as Madrid and Barcelona are the two largest cities in Spain, and they are often identified with "Spanish-ness" and Catalanism, respectively.

Why does AC Milan not call themselves AC Milano?

AC Milan was founded as a cricket club in 1899 by British expatriates Alfred Edwards and Herbert Kilpin, who came from the British city of Nottingham. In honor of its origins, the club has retained the English spelling of its city's name, instead of changing it to the Italian Milano

How did Juventus get their zebra-stripe jerseys?

The Turin-based Juventus FC have played in black-and-white striped shirts since 1903. Originally, they played in pink shirts with a black tie, but because continual washing faded the color, Juventus asked one of their team members, Englishman John Savage, if he had any contacts in England who could supply new shirts. Savage had a friend in Nottingham, who shipped them the jerseys worn by his favourite team, Notts County FC, which were zebra-striped. Juventus has worn them ever since.

What team holds the record for most consecutive championships in the French league's premier division?

Olympique Lyonnais, based in Lyon, won the premier league title seven years straight, from 2002–2008, a record that no other club in France has matched.

Who was Father Dewald?

On December 19, 1909, a group of young men gathered at a pub called Zum Wildschütz in the German city of Dortmund to form a new soccer club. They were unhappy with their church-sponsored Trinity Youth soccer club, where they played under the stern eye of the parish priest, Father Dewald. As they made their plans, the priest suddenly arrived to break up the meeting, but he was blocked at the door and prevented from entering. The new team would be called Borussia Dortmund, taking the name Borussia, which is Latin for Prussia, from the name of a nearby brewery. In later decades, the club Father Dewar tried to prevent would go on to win six German championships and in 1966 would become the first German team to win the European Cup.

Who were the "Irate Eight"?

Although the Football Association of Wales (FAW) is a voting member of FIFA, prior to 1992 Wales did not have its own football league. Because of this, some FAW member teams in northern Wales played within the English football league system (called the English pyramid). In 1992 the FAW formed the League of Wales (now called the Welsh Premier League) to better cement their position within FIFA. Eight Welsh teams playing within the English pyramid refused to join the new league. Those teams were Bangor City, Barry Town, Caernarfon Town, Colwyn Bay, Merthyr Tydfil, Newport County, Newtown, and Rhyl. They were called the Irate Eight because launched legal proceedings against the FAW fighting rules requiring them to play in the new league.

What is the oldest non-school soccer team in England?

Schools such as Eton and Cambridge were instrumental in establishing some of England's earliest soccer teams, but the Sheffield Football Club, in Sheffield, is England's oldest documented non-school soccer club, and was founded in 1857. It initially played a code of its own devising. The club joined the English Football Association (FA) in 1863 and is recognized by both the FA and FIFA as the world's oldest club now playing association football. The club's rules influenced the FA including handball, free kicks, corners, and throw-ins; it did not adopt the Association's code in full until 1877.

What does *Ludere Causa Ludendi* mean?

Queen's Park Football Club are an association football club based in Glasgow, Scotland. They are currently the only amateur club in the Scottish League and their amateur status is reflected by their motto, *Ludere Causa Ludendi* — "to play for the sake of playing."

What is the oldest soccer club in Ireland?

Cliftonville Football and Athletic Club, know as "the Reds," is a Northern Irish soccer team playing in the Irish Football Association's Premiership. Founded on September 20, 1879 by John McCredy McAlery in the north Belfast district of Cliftonville, it is the oldest football club in Ireland and celebrated its 125th anniversary in 2004.

What is the origin of Manchester United FC?

Teams that Founded the National Football League of Wales in 1992
- Abergavenny Thursdays
- Aberystwyth
- Afan Lido
- Bangor City
- Briton Ferry
- Caersws
- Conwy United
- Connahs Quay Nomads
- Cwmbran
- Ebbw Vale
- Flint Town United
- Haverfordwest County
- Holywell Town
- Inter Cardiff
- Llanelli
- Llanidloes
- Maesteg Park
- Mold Alexandra
- Newtown
- Porthmadog

Manchester United began life being called Newton Heath L&YR in 1878 when a group of workers from the Lancashire and Yorkshire Railways formed a soccer team. The club entered the Football League in 1892 and began to sever its links with the rail depot, becoming an independent company, appointing a club secretary and dropping the "L&YR" from their name to become simply Newton Heath FC. In 1902, a sizeable donation from J.H. Davies, the managing director of Manchester Breweries, saved the club from bankruptcy. The club required a change of name to reflect the fresh start and Manchester United was officially adopted on April 26, 1902.

Quickies
Did you know ...
- in their early days, while still called Newton Heath, the club that would eventually become Manchester United was nicknamed "The Heathens"?

Has Southampton FC always had that name?

Southampton FC was founded in 1885 by members of St. Mary's Church of England Young Men's Association and began life as St Mary's YMA. The club adopted the name Southampton St. Mary's when they joined England's Southern League in 1894. After they won the Southern League title in 1896–97, the club became a limited company and changed their name to Southampton FC.

What are the 22 founding teams of England's Premier League?

Arsenal, Aston Villa, Blackburn Rovers, Chelsea, Coventry City, Crystal Palace, Everton, Ipswich Town, Leeds United, Liverpool, Manchester City, Manchester United, Middlesborough, Norwich City, Nottingham Forest, Oldham Athletic, Queens Park Rangers, Sheffield United, Sheffield Wednesday, Southampton, Tottenham Hotspur, and Wimbledon.

What is the Merseyside Derby?

Quickies
Did you know ...
- Aston Villa's first match, held in 1874, was against the local Aston Brook St. Mary's Rugby team, and as a condition of the match, the Villa side had to agree to play the first half under rugby rules and the second half under soccer rules?

The Merseyside Derby is the name given to any match between the English teams Everton FC and Liverpool FC, the two most successful clubs from the city of Liverpool. Traditionally, the Merseyside Derby was referred to as The Friendly Derby because of the large number of families with supporters of both teams. It is one of the few local English soccer rivalries that does not enforce fan segregation at games.

How did Arsenal get their strange name?

Arsenal FC were founded as Dial Square in 1886 by workers at the Royal Arsenal in Woolwich, west of London, but they were renamed Royal Arsenal shortly afterwards. They changed their name to Woolwich Arsenal after turning professional in 1891. The club joined the English Football League in 1893, but low attendance led to financial problems leaving them effectively bankrupt by 1910, when they were taken over by Henry Norris. In 1913 Norris moved the team to the new Arsenal Stadium in Highbury, North London, and they dropped "Woolwich" from their name the following year.

Why do Tottenham Hotspur FC have a bird on their crest?

That bird is a cockerel, a fighting cock with a spur on its leg. In 1882 the Hotspur Football Club was formed by grammar schoolboys from the Bible class at All Hallows Church. They were also members of Hotspur Cricket Club and it is thought that the name Hotspur was associated with Sir Henry Percy, who was "Harry Hotspur" of Shakespeare's *Henry IV, Part I*, and who lived locally during in the fourteenth century. Harry Hotspur was famous for his riding spurs and fighting cocks. In 1884 the club was renamed Tottenham Hotspur Football and Athletic Club to distinguish itself from another team called London Hotspur.

> **Quickies**
> *Did you know ...*
> - in 2003, Chelsea FC was purchased by Russian oil magnate Roman Abramovich for £60 million?

Who founded Liverpool FC?

Liverpool FC was founded after a rent dispute between Everton FC and John Houlding, the leaseholder of Anfield, where Everton played. Houlding purchased Anfield outright in 1891, proposing an increase in the rent from £100 to £250 per year. Everton who had been playing at

World's Top Ten Richest Teams According to Forbes	
1. Manchester United	US$1,800 million (€1,333 million/£897 million)
2. Real Madrid	$1,285 million (€951 million/£640 million)
3. Arsenal	$1,200 million (€888 million/£598 million)
4. Liverpool	$1,050 million (€777 million/£523 million)
5. Bayern Munich	$917 million (€679 million/£457 million)
6. AC Milan	$798 million (€591 million/£398 million)
7. Barcelona	$784 million (€580 million/£391 million)
8. Chelsea	$764 million (€566 million/£381 million)
9. Juventus	$510 million (€378 million/£254 million)
10. Schalke 04	$470 million (€348 million/£234 million)

Anfield for seven years refused to meet his demands and moved to a new stadium in Goodison Park. Liverpool FC was founded by Houlding on March 15, 1892, to play at the vacated Anfield. The original name was to be Everton FC and Athletic Grounds, Ltd., or Everton Athletic for short, but it was changed to Liverpool FC when The Football Association refused to recognize the team as Everton.

Why Sheffield Wednesday and not Thursday or Monday?

Sheffield Wednesday was a cricket club when it originally formed in 1820 as The Wednesday Cricket Club — named after the day of the week when they played their matches. The cricketers formed the soccer branch of their club in 1867. The cricket branch eventually expired, but the name survived.

Quickies

Did you know ...

• Celtic were fined a record £100,000 in August 1994 for poaching manager Tommy Burns from Kilmarnock?

Who founded Rangers FC?

Two brothers, Peter and Moses McNeil, with the help of two friends, Peter Campbell and William McBeath, founded Rangers Football Club in 1872. The original name for the club was Argyle and possibly relates to the large numbers of Highlanders who moved to Glasgow during the Victorian era. The club moved to Ibrox in 1887.

Quickies

Did you know ...

- until 1989, when Mo Johnston signed for them, Rangers had never fielded a high-profile Catholic player?

Why are Glasgow's Rangers nicknamed the Teddy Bears?

Glasgow's Rangers are nicknamed the Teddy Bears, from the rhyming slang for "Gers," which in turn is short for Rangers.

Quickies

Did you know ...

- of the 11 clubs who formed the original Scottish League, only five are still league teams — Rangers, Celtic, Dumbarton, Hearts, and St. Mirren?

Why did Glasgow's Rangers have to scrap their new away jersey design in 2002?

The rivalry between Glasgow's Rangers and Celtic teams runs deep. Celtic were formed in 1888 by Irish Catholic immigrants who began emigrating to the West of Scotland in the 1840s. Rangers, who were formed in 1873, have always been perceived as "the Protestant club" and Celtic "the Catholic club." Orange, of course, is a symbolic colour of Protestantism, so when Rangers, whose traditional colours are blue and white, unwisely introduced a "tangerine" away jersey in the spring of 2002, it sparked an immediate outcry of sectarianism. By October there was such an uproar that they had to scrap the shirt.

Quickies

Did you know ...

- the first-ever Celtic goal was scored against Rangers by Neil McCallum in the club's inaugural match?

Who founded Celtic FC?

Celtic were founded at a meeting in St. Mary's Church Hall on East Rose Street (now Forbes Street), Calton, Glasgow, by Brother Walfrid, an Irish Marist brother, on November 6, 1887. The purpose stated in the official club records was stated as "being to alleviate poverty in Glasgow's

East End parishes." Walfrid's move to establish the club was a means of fundraising for his charity, The Poor Children's Dinner Table.

When did Rangers FC and Celtic FC first meet on the pitch?

On May 28, 1888, Celtic played their first official match, and it was against none other than Rangers — a club that had existed since 1872. Celtic won 5–2, fielding eight guest players from Hibernian FC.

Domestic Championships of the "Old Firm" Rangers

- *Scottish League Championships (51)*: 1891, 1899, 1900, 1901, 1902, 1911, 1912, 1913, 1918, 1920, 1921, 1923, 1924, 1925, 1927, 1928, 1929, 1930, 1931, 1933, 1934, 1935, 1937, 1939, 1947, 1949, 1950, 1953, 1956, 1957, 1959, 1961, 1963, 1964, 1975, 1976, 1978, 1987, 1989, 1990, 1991, 1992, 1993, 1994, 1995, 1996, 1997, 1999, 2000, 2003, 2005.
- *Scottish Cup winners (32)*: 1894, 1897, 1898, 1903, 1928, 1930, 1932, 1934, 1935, 1936, 1948, 1949, 1950, 1953, 1960, 1962, 1963, 1964, 1966, 1973, 1976, 1978, 1979, 1981, 1992, 1993, 1996, 1999, 2000, 2002, 2003, 2008.
- *League Cup winners (25)*: 1947, 1949, 1961, 1962, 1964, 1965, 1971, 1976, 1978, 1979, 1982, 1984, 1985, 1987, 1988, 1989, 1991, 1993, 1994, 1997, 1999, 2002, 2003, 2005, 2008.

Domestic Championships of the "Old Firm" Celtic

- *Scottish League Championships (42)*: 1893, 1894, 1896, 1898, 1905, 1906, 1907, 1908, 1909, 1910, 1914, 1915, 1916, 1917, 1919, 1922, 1926, 1936, 1938, 1954, 1966, 1967, 1968, 1969, 1970, 1971, 1972, 1973, 1974, 1977, 1979, 1981, 1982, 1986, 1988, 1998, 2001, 2002, 2004, 2006, 2007, 2008.
- *Scottish Cup (34)*: 1892, 1899, 1900, 1904, 1907, 1908, 1911, 1912, 1914, 1923, 1925, 1927, 1931, 1933, 1937, 1951, 1954, 1965, 1967, 1969, 1971, 1972, 1974, 1975, 1977, 1980, 1985, 1988, 1989, 1995, 2001, 2004, 2005, 2007.
- *Scottish League Cup (13)*: 1956–57, 1957–58, 1965–66, 1966–67, 1967–68, 1968–69, 1969–70, 1974–75, 1982–83, 1997–98, 1999–2000, 2000/01, 2005–06.

Who were the Lisbon Lions?

The Lisbon Lions is the nickname given to the Celtic team that won the European Cup at the Estádio Nacional in Lisbon, Portugal on May 25, 1967, defeating Inter Milan 2–1. The squad was one of only two clubs ever to win the competition with a team composed entirely of players from the club's home country (the other was Steaua Bucharest of Romania in 1986). All the members of this Celtic team were born within 30 miles (48 kilometres) of Glasgow.

What was the first non-U.S. Major League soccer team?

That would be the Toronto FC, which was formed in 2006 and plays at BMO Field on the grounds of the Canadian National Exhibition. The team set an MLS record in season ticket sales, selling 14,000 before they'd even appeared in a game.

Why did Houston Dynamo have to change their name?

The Houston franchise of the MLS was officially formed in 2005 and announced their name in January 2006 as Houston 1836. The number, stated the league and team owners, referred to the founding

Quickies
Did you know ...
- Vale of Leven FC managed to play the entire 22 games of their 1891–92 season without winning any of them?

The Scottish league's Founding Members, From 1890-91
- Abercorn
- Cambuslang
- Celtic
- Cowlairs
- Dumbarton
- Heart of Midlothian
- Rangers
- Renton
- St. Mirren
- Third Lanark
- Vale of Leven

Quickies
Did you know ...
- most players in Major League Soccer (MLS), the North American men's pro league, would have to play two years to earn what David Beckham makes in one game?

Quickies
Did you know ...
- the Columbus Crew was the first team to officially join the MLS league, and the first to have a stadium built specifically for MLS soccer?

Quickies

Did you know ...

- the New England Revolution lost the MLS Cup final three years running, from 2005 to 2007?

Quickies

Did you know ...

- the Chicago Fire won both the MLS Cup and the U.S Open Cup in their first year of play, 1997?

year of Houston and was chosen after an Internet fan survey. Many Mexican-Americans, however, were offended by the choice since the year 1836 is also associated with the bitter Texan War of Independence from Mexico. After realizing their blunder had inadvertently offended many of the state's most devoted soccer fans, the league and ownership changed the name to Houston Dynamo in March 2006.

soccer talk

Where does the word "soccer" come from?

Most people believe that the name "soccer" is an Americanization, but they are wrong. England's Football Association was formed in London in October 1863. The new rules set down by the FA prohibited the carrying of the ball, and as such, the name "association football" was coined to distinguish the game from rugby. By 1889, "association football" had been abbreviated in common use to "socca," with the spelling soccer appearing first in 1895.

What are pinnies?

Pinnies are the colourful mesh vests used in children's soccer, worn over clothes to distinguish which team a player is on. The word is an abbreviation of pinafore, which is a child's apron-like gown with sleeves worn to protect clothing. Pinafores were originally closed in the front — or afore — with a pin, hence the name.

Where is futsal played?

Futsal is played indoors. It is a version of association football. Its name is derived from the Portuguese *futebol de salão* and the Spanish *fútbol de salón*, which can be translated as "indoor football."

When could a team score a golden goal?

The "golden goal" of soccer was once referred to as "sudden death." If a game in a knockout tournament was tied at the end of regulation time, extra time would be added and as soon as a team scored during that extra time, they were declared winners and the match was over. The extra-time goal was called the "golden goal" because of its value. Although records show the sudden-death method had been in use in soccer since

1868, the term "golden goal" was introduced by FIFA in 1993 because the term "sudden death" was perceived to have negative connotations. After the 2004 European Cup, the golden goal was officially removed from the Laws of the Game, which now indicate that ties are to be settled using two extra periods, not exceeding 15 minutes each. If a tie still exists after extra time, a shootout is used to settle the game.

What does "play the whistle" mean?

Just because the assistant referee holds up an offside flag, it does not mean play has stopped. On an offside call, play only stops when the referee blows the whistle. That is why coaches tell their players to "play the whistle and not the flag," meaning even if you see an offside flag, keep going until you hear the whistle because the referee may be giving you advantage.

What is an offside trap?

The offside trap is a tactic in which the defenders wait until the last possible moment, then take a large step upfield in order to throw their opponents into an offside position. It must be carefully timed so that the step forward is made before the ball is played. It also relies heavily upon having an alert assistant referee who will be looking at the second-last defender, and not looking upfield when the ball is played.

What happens if a player is charged with "going in with studs up"?

Even with shin guards for protection, being on the business end of a set of soccer cleats is never a pleasant experience. When a player raises his feet above the level of the ball when tackling, especially when sliding, it can threaten serious injury to another player's legs. Called "going in with studs up," this sort of unsporting play — controlled or otherwise — should be immediately noticed by any referee worth his salt and the player shown a yellow or red card, depending on the severity of the infraction.

What are calf dimples?

This is the name given by players to the small holes or indentations left in the skin after someone comes in "studs up" from behind and their cleats dig into your calf.

What does "bend it like Beckham" mean?

The phrase "bend it like Beckham" was popularized as the title of a British movie from 2002, starring Parminder Nagra and Keira Knightley. The title refers to David Beckham's ability to put spin on a ball from a free kick, causing it to curve — or "bend" — in trajectory arund the defence and into the net. Nagra's character in the film, Jess Bhamra, shows a similar aptitude for bending free kicks.

What does "bank it like Beckham" mean?

The term "to bend" a soccer ball means to put spin on a ball from a free kick to give it a curving trajectory around defenders. The phrase "bank it like Beckham mean" is a joke on this phrase, playing on the title of the feature film *Bend it like Beckham*, and referring to Beckham's ability to land copious amounts of money in the bank upon signing a US$250-million deal with the Los Angeles Galaxy.

What term did N.L. Jackson, founder of Corinthians FC, give to soccer?

On May 10, 1886, N.L. Jackson, founder of Corinthians FC and assistant secretary of England's Football Association, proposed that all players taking part for England in international matches should be "presented with a white silk cap with red rose embroidered on the front." Caps are no longer given today, but the term has lived on, so that if a player has participated in 10 international matches, it is said he has 10 caps.

What is a friendly?

This is a non-competition game, the results of which do not count for standings in a league of tournament. The two sides are just having a friendly game.

What is a dummy?

This is a pass trick pass intended to fool the defence. A pass is made to a player who then allows the ball to roll through his legs — without touching it — to another player.

Why is it said that soccer players dribble?

The word dribble dates back to the sixteenth century when it was used, as it is now, to describe a flow of drips or drops — though back then drips and drops were called "dribs." It was first used in relation to soccer in 1863 by British journalist A.G. Guillemard, who described an Eton player "dribbling the ball slowly forward before his feet" in the October issue of *The Sporting Gazette*. The term describes skillful movement of the ball upfield in short, small kicks.

The Four "Drops" of Soccer

- *Drop ball* — a method of restart in which the referee "drops" the ball to the ground. The players may not kick the ball until the ball touches the ground.
- *Drop kick* — a punting method the goalkeeper uses where he drops the ball to the ground, then kicks the ball just after it hits the ground.
- *Drop off* — to move farther away from one's mark. Issued as an instruction to a player from the coach or another player.
- *Drop pass* — a player passes the ball behind himself to a teammate, or leaves the ball for a teammate.

When is a soccer player like a jockey?

When they are delaying the forward progress of an opponent with the ball by holding a position close to and goal-side of the opponent so that he can be tackled once support arrives. Sorry, no horses allowed on the pitch.

When is a soccer player like a juggler?

Juggling is act of keeping a soccer ball off the ground by a single person or a group of people. It can be part of a game, or a game unto itself. All body parts may be used except the arms and hands.

When is a soccer player like a boxer?

Unless you are talking about a serious foul — and in the heat of play, fist fights do sometimes break out — then it can only be the goaltender, whose legal play of hitting the ball with a closed fist is called punching.

When is a soccer player like a diver?

When he tries to fool the referee by exaggerating the effect of contact with another player. It usually entails writhing on the ground in an undignified state of mock agony. Such unsporting behavior is called diving and is punishable by yellow card.

What is a tackle?

Unlike American football, bringing another player to the ground is a no-no in soccer. To tackle another player means to take the ball from him with your feet. In soccer, you tackle the ball, not the player.

What is a square ball?

No, it is not a cube. Such a ball shape would not work well for soccer — or any other game! A square ball is one passed on the ground in a line parallel to the touchlines on the pitch.

What is a 50/50 ball?

This is a loose ball contested by a player from each team and which may be won by either one of them. There is a 50/50 chance of it going to either team.

When is a player "ball side"?

A player who is closer to the ball than to the opponent he is playing against is said to be "ball side" of the opponent.

What is booking?

This is an officiating term used to indicate that a player has had his name/number recorded by the referee for receiving a yellow or red card. The player is said to have been "booked."

What does it mean to be "caught square"?

While this can mean that someone notices that you are a nerd, in soccer it means that two or more defenders have been beaten by a through ball because they were positioned square to one another in a line across the field parallel to the goal line. Of course, there are no nerds in soccer.

Where is the channel?

The Three Cs of Ball Control
- *Chop* — forceful kick to redirect the ball used to flee a defender.
- *Cross* — a kick from the near the touchline across the front of the goal.
- *Cut* — a subtle kick to move the ball in a different direction.

The channel is imaginary lane about 10 yards (9.15 metres) wide, running the length of the field and located about 10 yards in from the touchline. It is often exploited for diagonal runs by wing- and centre-forwards, who look for a through ball to be played along it.

What is a flat back formation?

Quickies
Did you know ...
- because of its shape, the penalty arc is often called the "D"?

This is a defensive formation where the back three or four defenders move in tandem, maintaining a line straight across the field.

What does it mean to say the ball has gone into touch?

It means it is dead, because it has crossed the touchlines. When the ball goes into the area outside of the field of play, beyond the touchlines, it may be legally touched by a player's hands, so the term means that the ball has gone into that area.

What does it mean to mark a player?

This is when a defender is assigned to cover a particular opponent player. The player being guarded is the mark.

What is a nutmeg?

This is not one of the Spice Girls. This is the action of putting a ball through the space created when a defender has his legs spread. A player is said to have been "nutmegged" or "megged."

What is a punt?

Quickies
Did you know ...
- assigning a defender to mark a dangerous attacker closely is called shadow-marking?

A method of kicking that goalkeepers use to clear the ball upfield, wherein the ball is dropped from the hand and kicked before touching the ground. The goalkeeper has six seconds after picking up the ball to punt it or release it.

What does it mean to push?

This is when players on one team collectively move forward towards the opponents' goal in order to put opponents in an offside position. As an instruction bellowed from pitchside by a coach, it can take a few different forms, including "push up," "push out," "out," "step," "step up," and even "pull."

Quickies
Did you know ...
- in the UK, a soccer game is often called a "match," a "fixture," or a "tie"?

What is a shootout?

While there have been documented hooligan incidents of gunfire at soccer games, a shootout is actually a tie-breaking device that pits one player against the goalkeeper in either penalty kicks or a breakaway-type run from 35 yards (32 metres) away. In both cases, the winning team is determined after a best of five chances alternating with each team. If tied after five, the contest continues with different players until one team scores and the other team doesn't.

What is a player's strip?

No, that's not when a player lifts his shirt over his head after a goal. It is the term for the uniform worn by all team members, consisting of jersey, shorts, and stockings. As with most pro sports, teams will often have both a home strip in the club colors and a contrasting away strip. The goalkeeper wears a distinctive uniform often referred to as a team goalkeeper strip.

What is time lost?

The referee has the ability to add time at the end of either half for time lost because of treatment or removal of injured players, wasted time, substitutions, or any other cause.

Where is the upper V?

The upper V, also called the upper 90, is the intersection of the crossbar and goalpost.

What is a banana kick?

This is a type of kick that gives the ball a curved trajectory — a bend like a banana — used to get the ball around a goaltender or defender.

What is a bicycle kick?

This is a highly entertaining acrobatic shot. A player kicks the ball in mid-air backwards and over his own head, usually making contact above

Soccer Acronyms

AFC — Asian Football Confederation
APSL — American Professional Soccer League
AYSO — American Youth Soccer Organization
CAF — *Confédération Africaine de Football*
CONCACAF —*Confederation Norte-Centroamericana y Del Caribe de Football*
CONMEBOL — *Confederación Sudamericana de Fútbol*
CSA — Canadian Soccer Association
FA — Football Association (England)
FAI — Football Association of Ireland
FAW — Football Association of Wales
FIFA — *Fédération Internationale de Football Association*
IFA — Irish Football Association (Northern Ireland)
IFAB — International Football Association Board
IFFHS — International Federation of Football History and Statistics
MISL — Major Indoor Soccer League
MLS — Major League Soccer
NASL — North American Soccer League
OFC — Oceania Football Confederation
SFA — Scottish Football Association
UEFA — *Union des Associations Européennes de Football*
USSF — United States Soccer Federation
USYSA — United States Youth Soccer Association
WSF — Women's Soccer Federation

waist level. It is so named because the player's legs spin as though on a bicycle. It is also called the scissors kick.

What is a wall?

This is the term for the line of players who stand between the ball and their own goal when a free kick is going to be taken. These players form a human barrier between the ball and their goal.

What is a super-sub?

This is not the giant sandwich you eat while watching your favourite team on TV. The term "super-sub" refers to a substitution player who saves the game by scoring a winning goal.

Who called soccer "The Beautiful Game"?

The phrase "The Beautiful Game" as a synonym for soccer was first coined by Didi (Waldyr Pereira), a Brazilian superstar soccer player. The Brazilian Portuguese expression *Joga Bonito* (to "play beautifully") parallels this phrase. In 1977 Pelé, one of soccer's greatest superstars, named his autobiography *My Life and the Beautiful Game.*

soccer culture

Why did David Beckham turn down an appearance on *The Simpsons*?

In a 2004 episode of *The Simpsons*, Marge Simpson makes a Christmas speech mocking David Beckham for an alleged extramarital affair. Apparently Boy Spice didn't think to laugh and when an offer came for him to do a cameo in Springfield, he turned them down.

Have any professional soccer players appeared on *The Simpsons*?

Yes, Brazilian star Ronaldo appeared on *The Simpsons* in episode 17 of season 18, titled "Marge Gamer." Or rather, an animated drawing of him appeared telling Homer that his daughter, Lisa, was a "flopper" (a.k.a.: diver) in her soccer game and causing Homer to red-card her. It was Ronaldo's real voice.

Film's and TV Shows Pelé Has Acted In
- *Os Estranhos* (1969) (TV series)
- *Barão Otelo no Barato dos Bilhões* (1971)
- *A Marcha* (1973)
- *Os Trombadinhas* (1979)
- *Escape to Victory* (1981)
- *A Minor Miracle* (1983)
- *Pedro Mico* (1985)
- *Os Trapalhões e o Rei do Futebol* (1986)
- *Hotshot* (1987)
- *Solidão, Uma Linda História de Amor* (1989)

What creative endeavours has Pelé engaged in since retiring?

Pelé has published several autobiographies, starred in documentary and semi-documentary films, and composed various musical pieces, including the entire soundtrack for the film *Pelé* in 1977. He has acted in fictional TV shows and films, most notably appearing alongside other footballers of the 1960s and 1970s, Michael Caine, and Sylvester Stallone, in the 1981 film *Escape to Victory*, about an attempted escape from a Second World War Nazi POW Camp. Pelé was also the first sports figure featured in a video game with the Atari 2600 game "Pelé's Soccer."

158

What is Gloria 03?

The 1942 German film *Das große Spiel* ("The Big Game"), tells the story of a football team called Gloria 03. It was directed by Robert A. Stemmle and scenes set at a soccer final match were filmed at the actual 1941 German championship final between Rapid Wien versus FC Schalke 04.

Quickies
Did you know ...
- the Kansas City Wizards are named after *The Wizard of Oz*?

Who wrote the song "Coup de Boule"?

"Coup de Boule" was written and performed by brothers Sébastien and Emmanuel Lipszyc, along with Franck Lascombes. The humorous soca-style song is about Zinedine Zidane's career-ending head-butt of Marco Materazzi at the 2006 FIFA World Cup final. The song parodies another by French TV and radio host Sébastien Cauet, titled "Zidane y va marquer."

When was the first radio broadcast of a soccer game?

On January 22, 1927, Arsenal played Sheffield United to a 1–1 draw in a Division One match at Highbury. It was the first match ever covered by radio, as the BBC called the game from pitch-side.

What was the first FA final to be broadcast on radio?

The first FA Cup final to be broadcast was the historic match between the Welsh side Cardiff City and Arsenal on April 23, 1927. It was a meeting of firsts that day, as Cardiff, in a 1–0 victory, became the first team from outside England to have ever won the cup. No team has done it since.

Top Ten Soccer Movies
- *Escape to Victory* (1981)
- *Bend It Like Beckham* (2002)
- *Das Wunder von Bern (The Miracle of Bern)* (2003)
- *My Name is Joe* (1998)
- *Mean Machine* (2001)
- *The Match* (1999)
- *Ladybugs* (1992)
- *When Saturday Comes* (1996)
- *A Shot at Glory* (2000)
- *Phörpa (The Cup)* (1999)

When was the first television transmission of a soccer game?

In 1937 the BBC was on hand to televise, for the first time, portions of the FA Cup final between Preston North End and Sunderland from Wembley Stadium in London. The following year, the BBC televised the entire match.

Has the story of the historic German 1954 World Cup champions ever been put on film?

Yes, Söhnke Wortmann's 2003 German box-office hit *Das Wunder von Bern* (*The Miracle of Bern*) retells the story of the German team's route to victory through the eyes of a young boy.

Who were Mitchell & Kenyon?

The Mitchell & Kenyon film company was a pioneer of early commercial movies. Based in Blackburn in Lancashire, England, at the start of the twentieth century they were best known for minor fictional narrative films. In 1994, a hoard of 800 Mitchell & Kenyon film negatives were discovered and restored. Amongst this collection are numerous films documenting soccer matches between English FA teams just after the turn of the century. The films are in storage at the British Film Institute, but can be viewed on YouTube (http://www.youtube.com).

Top Ten Worst Soccer Movies
- *Siu lam juk kau (Shaolin Soccer)* (2001)
- *Soccer Mom* (2008)
- *Soccer Dog: The Movie* (1999)
- *Soccer Dog: European Cup* (2004)
- *Mad About Mambo* (2000)
- *Switching Goals* (1999)
- *The Big Green* (1995)
- *Her Best Move* (2007)
- *Air Bud: World Pup* (2000)
- *Kicking and Screaming* (2005)

Early Matches Caught on Film by Mitchell & Kenyon
- Newcastle vs. Liverpool, 1901 (1:55 minutes)
- Rotherham Town vs. Thornhill, 1902 (1:24 minutes)
- Everton vs. Liverpool Merseyside Derby, 1902 (2:10 minutes)
- Burnley vs. Manchester United, 1902 (1:49 minutes)
- Sheffield United vs. Bury, 1902 (2:23 minutes)
- Rotherham vs. Thornhill, 1902 (1:42 minutes)
- Notts County vs. Middlesbrough, 1902 (2:50 minutes)
- Bradford City vs. Gainsborough Trinity, 1903 (3:19 minutes)
- Preston North End vs. Wolverhampton Wanderers, 1904 (1:57 minutes)
- Blackburn Rovers vs. Aston Villa, 1904 (1:28 minutes)
- Preston North End vs. Aston Villa, 1905 (2:22 minutes)
- Sunderland vs. Leicester Fosse, 1907 (1:16 minutes)

Why is there a soccer magazine in Holland called *Nummer 14*?

The popular Dutch soccer magazine *Nummer 14* (*Number 14*) takes its name from the number worn by Johan Cruijff, considered by most to have been Holland's greatest player.

What is TOOFIF?

Quickies
Did you know ...
- Celtic began publishing *The Celtic View*, Great Britain's oldest club magazine in football, in 1965.

TOOFIF stands for "There's Only One F in Fulham," which is the title of an independently owned fanzine dedicated to Fulham Football Club. It is edited by David Lloyd, published six times per year and was founded in 1988.

What are WAGs?

WAGs is an acronym created by the British tabloid press to mean Soccer "wives and girlfriends." The acronym has been in use since 1994, but

WAGS and Their Stags Who Have Made the Broadsheets	
WAG	STAG
Victoria Beckham	David Beckham
Cheryl Cole	Ashley Cole
Coleen Rooney	Wayne Rooney
Carly Zucker	Joe Cole
Alex Curran	Steven Gerrard
Melanie Slade	Theo Walcott
Elen Rives	Frank Lampard

became extremely popular during the 2006 World Cup, in Germany, when the press gave increasing gossip coverage to the socializing and shopping activities of the English WAGs, who were based in the German town of Baden Baden.

What is *Panini*?

These are not something you eat at an Italian soccer game. *Panini* is the brand name of an Italian firm that produces collectable stickers. The company is based in Modena and named after the Panini brothers, who founded it in 1961. It became famous in the 1960s for its soccer collections, which can now sometimes reach very high prices on the collectors' market. The slogan "Stick with Panini" could once be heard in a jingle following the television advertisements that Panini aired during children's programming.

Top Ten Soccer Books
- *Fever Pitch*, Nick Hornby
- *Among the Thugs*, Bill Buford
- *Brilliant Orange: The Neurotic Genius of Dutch Soccer*, David Winner
- *Soccer in Sun and Shadow*, Edward Galeano
- *How Soccer Explains the World*, Franklin Foer
- *The Soccer War*, Ryszard Kapuscinski
- *Foul! The Secret World of FIFA*, Andrew Jennings
- *Congratulations, You Have Just Met the ICF*, Cass Pennant
- *Futebol, the Brazillian Way of Life*, Alex Bellos
- *Now You Know Soccer*, Doug Lennox

What is a derby?

Derby matches, or matches between two neighbouring rival clubs, are often fiercely competitive and provide a spectacle in football for the supporters. Sometimes there are underlying political and sectarian tensions, such as the Protestant versus Catholic tensions between Glasgow's Rangers and Celtic. The term often applies to matches between two local teams from the same city or region, but it is also sometimes used to refer to matches between big clubs from the same country, such as FC Barcelona and Real Madrid.

What are ultras?

Ultras are a sanctioned form of team supporters renowned for their fanatical and elaborate displays. They are predominantly European and South American followers of soccer teams. Ultras frequently display their support through choreographed performances called *tifos* and also through "terrace chants," which are sung en masse, often to well-known tunes, but with the words changed.

Traditional Football Foods
- Steak and kidney pies (England)
- Meat and potato pies (England)
- Bovril broth (England)
- *Sanduíche de calabresa* (pepperoni sandwich) (Brazil)
- *Feijão tropeiro* (beans and sausage) (Brazil)
- Bratwurst and beer (Germany)
- *Choripán* (grilled chorizo and crusty bread) (Argentina)
- *Pap* (maize porridge), *braai* (BBQ), *idombolo* (dumplings) (Johannesburg)

What are *tifos*?

Tifo was originally the Italian word for the phenomenon of supporting a sport team, but it is now mainly used as the name for the sort of spectacular, choreographed display staged by large groups of fans called "ultras" on the balconies or terraces, of arenas or stadiums during sporting events, most often soccer matches. For example, *tifos* can consist of large sections of the crown holding and turning colour placards, to create larger "tiled" banners. Other materials that have been used include coloured plastic sheeting, flags, balloons, confetti, paper rolls, flares, fireworks, dolls, and mascots.

What is a firm?

A football firm, also known as a hooligan firm, is a gang formed to fight with the supporters of other teams. Their violent activity ranges from shouts and fist fights, to riots in which opposing firms clash with weaponry such as bats, bottles, rocks, or even knives and guns. In some cases, stadium brawls have caused fans to flee in panic, and fans have been killed when fences or walls have collapsed. In the most extreme cases,

Some Traditional Team Chants

- **Arsenal** — "One Nil, to the Arsenal," "She Wore a Yellow Ribbon," "Ooh to be a Gooner," "We're on Our Way," "Good Old Arsenal," "B'Jesus Said Paddy."
- **Aston Villa** — "Paul McGrath My Lord" (sung to the tune of "Kumbaya"), "Gabby Gabby Gabby Gabby Gabby Agbonlahor. He's Fast as Fuck" (sung to "Karma Chameleon").
- **Blackpool** — "Glad All Over," "Back Henry Street," "We are the Nutters, We Come From the Sea."
- **Celtic** — "The Celtic Song," "The Fields of Athenry," "Hampden in the Sun," "Celtic Symphony."
- **Inter Milan** — "C'é Solo L'Inter," "Pazza Inter."
- **Juventus** — "Juve, storia di un grande amore," "E' bianconero," "Juventuslandia," "Magica Juve," "Vecchia Signora," "Il cielo è bianconero."
- **Leeds United** — "Marching On Together," "Leeds United Calypso," "Glory, Glory Leeds United."
- **Liverpool** — "You'll Never Walk Alone," "The Fields of Anfield Road," "Poor Scouser Tommy."
- **Manchester United** — "Manchester United Calypso," "The Flowers of Manchester," "Molly Malone," "From the Dark Snows of Munich," "A Plaque at Man United," "Glory Glory Man United."
- **Rangers** — "Follow Follow," "Rule Britannia," "Billy Boys," "Every Other Saturday."
- **AS Roma** — "Roma, Roma, Roma," "Grazie Roma."
- **Sheffield United** — "The Greasy Chip Butty Song" (to the tune of "Annie's Song" by John Denver).
- **Tottenham Hotspur** — "It's A Grand Old Team To Play For," "I Can't Smile Without You."
- **Toronto FC** — "Danny Dichio."
- **Wolverhampton Wanderers** — "Those Were the Days," "I was Born on a Wanderer's Scarf," "Ring of Fire."

firm members, police, and bystanders have been killed in the violence, and riot police have intervened with tear gas, armoured vehicles, and water cannons.

Firms in England

Team	Firm
Aldershot	A Company
Arsenal	Gooners, The Herd
Aston Villa	Villa Youth, Steamers, Villa Hardcore, C-Crew
Birmingham City	Zulus
Blackpool	The Muckers
Bolton Wanderers	Cuckoo Boys
Bradford City	The Ointment
Brentford	Hounslow Mentals
Bristol City	City Service Firm
Burnley	Suicide Squad
Carlisle United	Border City Firm
Charlton Athletic	B Mob
Chelsea	Headhunters
Coventry	City The Legion
Derby County	Derby Lunatic Fringe
Everton County	Road Cutters
Grimsby Town	Cleethorpes Beach Patrol
Huddersfield Town	Huddersfield Young Casuals
Hull City	Hull City Psychos
Leeds United	Leeds United Service Crew
Leicester City	Baby Squad
Liverpool	The Urchins
Luton Town	The MIGs
Manchester City	Guvnors
Manchester United	The Red Army
Middlesbrough	The Frontline
Millwall	Bushwackers
Newcastle United FC	Newcastle Gremlins
Nottingham Forest FC	Forest Executive Crew
Norwich City	Norwich Hit Squad
Oldham Athletic	Fine Young Casuals
Plymouth Argyle	The Central Element
Portsmouth	6.57 Crew
Preston North End	Preston Para Squad
Queens Park Rangers	Bushbabies
Sheffield United	Blades Business Crew
Sheffield Wednesday	Owls Crime Squad
Southend United	CS Crew
Stoke City	Naughty Forty
Sunderland	Seaburn Casuals
Swindon Town	The Aggro Boys; Swindon Active Service (SAS)
Tottenham Hotspur	Yid Army
West Bromwich Albion	Section Five
West Ham United	Inter City Firm
Wolverhampton Wanderers	Subway Army

Firms in Scotland	
Team	Firm
Aberdeen	Aberdeen Soccer Casuals
Airdrie United	Section B
Celtic	Celtic Soccer Crew
Dundee and Dundee United FC	The Utility
Heart of Midlothian	Casual Soccer Firm
Hibernian	Capital City Service
Motherwell	Saturday Service
Rangers	Inter City Firm

What are casuals?

Casuals are a subculture of football culture that developed in the late 1970s and early 1980s in the United Kingdom, and is typified by hooliganism and the wearing of expensive European clothing by some hooligan firms. The subculture originated when many hooligans started wearing designer labels and expensive sportswear to avoid the attention of police. They didn't wear team colours, so it was easier to infiltrate rival groups and to enter pubs.

What is terrace retro?

The balcony seating area in a soccer stadium in the UK is called the terrace section. Terrace retro is a contemporary fashion movement that aims to revive the styles associated with young people who frequented the terrace sections of Merseyside clubs — in particular Liverpool — stadiums in the late 1970s and early 1980s.

What's the earliest instance of football hooliganism on record?

The first recorded instances of football hooliganism took place in the 1880s in England, when gangs of supporters would intimidate neighbourhoods, and attack referees and opposing supporters and players. In 1885, after Preston North End beat Aston Villa 5–0 in a friendly match, the two teams were pelted with stones, attacked with sticks, punched, kicked and spat at. One Preston player lost consciousness.

The following year, Preston fans fought Queen's Park fans in a railway station — the first recorded instance of football hooliganism away from a match.

What is a pitch invasion?

Called "rushing the field" in North America, a pitch invasion occurs when the fans at a soccer match spill onto the pitch, usually compelled by feeling of joy after their teem has won a major match, or feelings of rage after their team has lost. They used to be much more common than they are now at top-level soccer games, due to the fact that security was not as tight in the past as it is now.

What is the largest instance of death related to a soccer match?

On May 24, 1964, more than 300 soccer fans died and another 500 were injured in Lima, Peru, in a riot during an Olympic qualifying match between Argentina and Peru.

What was the Ibrox Disaster of 1971?

In the afternoon January 2, 1971, Rangers were playing Celtic at Glasgow's Ibrox Stadium. In the 89th minute, Celtic Jimmy Johnstone scored to break a 0–0 deadlock. Moments later, Ranger Colin Stein put

Famous Pitch Invasions

- *Celtic vs. Rangers* (1909) Scottish Cup final. At the end of a drawn replay the crowd invaded the pitch to protest at the lack of a result and at the prospect of having to pay to watch a third game. A riot ensued and the SFA withheld the cup.
- *Celtic vs. Internazionale Milano FC* (1967) European Cup. As the final whistle blew, fans of Celtic flooded the pitch in jubilation as Celtic became the first British team to lift the European Cup.
- *England vs. Scotland* (1977) Home International, Wembley. Scotland won 2–1. Scotland supporters invaded the pitch and destroyed one of the goals. The scenes were broadcast live on British television, and this is identified as one of the key moments when football hooliganism caught the interest of politicians.
- *Brighton vs. York* (1996). Fifteen minutes into this match, a mass invasion of supporters of both teams protesting the Brighton board's decision to sell Albion's Goldstone Ground caused the match to be abandoned.
- *Watford vs. Luton Town* (2002) Worthington Cup. Ten minutes before the game kicked off, Luton fans invaded the pitch, provokingthe Watford fans to do the same and resulting in a mass brawl on the pitch between the two sets of supporters. The game was delayed for 25 minutes before riot police regained order.
- *Reading vs. Derby County* (2006) Football League Championship. Reading beat Derby County 5–0 to claim the championship title one week after gaining promotion to the English Premiership for the first time in their 135-year history. In all 15,000 fans ran on the pitch, although no arrests were made.
- *Stoke vs. Leicester* (2008) Football League Championship. After a 0–0 draw at the Britannia Stadium proved enough to confirm Stoke City's return to the top flight of the English football league for the first time in 23 years, 18,000 jubilant Stoke fans flooded the pitch.

the equalizer in the Celtic net. As fans were leaving the stadium, barriers on a stairway gave way, causing a massive pileup of spectators. Sixty-six people were killed in the crush and over 200 were injured.

Famous Soccer Matches With Mass Fatalities

- Argentina 1968 — Crowds attending a match in Buenos Aires stampede after youths throw burning paper: over 70 people die.
- Nigeria 1979 — Crowds stampede during a floodlight failure: 24 fans die and 27 are injured.
- Moscow 1982 — Departing fans try to re-enter the stands after a last-minute goal in a UEFA Cup tie between Moscow Spartak and Dutch side Haarlem at the Luzhniki stadium: some media report up to 340 people are crushed to death, though the Soviet government newspaper *Izvestia* puts the death toll at 66.
- England 1985 — Fire engulfs the main stand at Valley Parade stadium: 56 people die and more than 200 are injured.
- Belgium 1985 — Rioting breaks out before the European Cup final between Italy's Juventus and English club Liverpool at the Heysel Stadium: 39 fans die.
- Nepal 1988 — Fans stampede toward locked exits during a hailstorm at Nepal's national soccer stadium: 70 people die.
- England 1989 — A crowd surge crushes packed fans against barriers at the English FA Cup semifinal match between Liverpool and Nottingham Forest at the Hillsborough stadium: 95 people are killed and at least 200 injured.
- Kenya 1991 — Crowds stampede during an African Nations' Cup qualifying match between Kenya and Mozambique: one fan is killed and 24 injured.
- Guatemala City 1996 — An avalanche of fans tumbles down seats and stairs in the terraces above a World Cup qualifying match between Guatemala and Costa Rica: 82 people die and at least 147 are injured.
- Liberia 1996 — Government troops open fire to stop pro- and anti-Gadafi sentiments being expressed during a game between Al Ahli and Al Ittihad: eight fans were killed and 39 injured.
- Democratic Republic of Congo 1998 — Government troops open fire in Kinshasa at a match between Vita Club and Motema Pembe at the Stade De Martyrs: four fans die.

finals and results

World Cup Finals Results

Year	Winner	Runners-Up	Result
1930	Uruguay	Argentina	4–2
1934	Italy	Czechoslovakia	2–1
1938	Italy	Hungary	4–2
1950	Uruguay	Brazil	2–1
1954	Germany	Hungary	3–2
1958	Brazil	Sweden	5–2
1962	Brazil	Czechoslovakia	3–1
1966	England	Germany	4–2
1970	Brazil	Italy	4–1
1974	Germany	Netherlands	2–1
1978	Argentina	Netherlands	3–1
1982	Italy	Germany	3–1
1986	Argentina	Germany	3–2
1990	Germany	Argentina	1–0
1994	Brazil	Italy	0–0 aet (3–2 penalty shootout)
1998	France	Brazil	3–0
2002	Brazil	Germany	2–0
2006	Italy	France	1–1 aet (5–3 penalty shootout)

FA Cup Finals Results

Year	Winner	Runners-Up	Result
1872	Wanderers	Royal Engineers	1–0
1873	Wanderers	Oxford University	2–0
1874	Oxford University	Royal Engineers	2–0
1875	Royal Engineers	Old Etonians	1–1 aet (2–0 replay)
1876	Wanderers	Old Etonians	1–1 aet (3–0 replay)

Year	Winner	Runners-Up	Result
1877	Wanderers	Oxford University	2–1 aet
1878	Wanderers	Royal Engineers	3–1
1879	Old Etonians	Clapham Rovers	1–0
1880	Clapham Rovers	Oxford University	1–0
1881	Old Carthusians	Old Etonians	3–0
1882	Old Etonians	Blackburn Rovers	1–0
1883	Blackburn Olympic	Old Etonians	2–1 aet
1884	Blackburn Rovers	Queens Park, Glasgow	2–1
1885	Blackburn Rovers	Queens Park, Glasgow	2–0
1886	Blackburn Rovers	West Bromwich Albion	0–0 aet (2–0 replay)
1887	Aston Villa	West Bromwich Albion	2–0
1888	West Bromwich	Albion Preston North End	2–1
1889	Preston North End	Wolverhampton Wanderers	3–0
1890	Blackburn Rovers	Sheffield Wednesday	6–1
1891	Blackburn Rovers	Notts County	3–1
1892	West Bromwich	Albion Aston Villa	3–0
1893	Wolverhampton	Wanderers Everton	1–0
1894	Notts County	Bolton Wanderers	4–1
1895	Aston Villa	West Bromwich Albion	1–0
1896	Sheffield Wednesday	Wolverhampton Wanderers	2–1
1897	Aston Villa	Everton	3–2
1898	Nottingham Forest	Derby County	3–1
1899	Sheffield United	Derby County	4–1
1900	Bury	Southampton	4–0
1901	Tottenham Hotspur	Sheffield United	2–2 aet (3–1 replay)

Year	Winner	Runners-Up	Result
1902	Sheffield United	Southampton	1–1 aet (2–1 replay)
1903	Bury	Derby County	6–0
1904	Manchester City	Bolton Wanderers	1–0
1905	Aston Villa	Newcastle United	2–0
1906	Everton	Newcastle United	1–0
1907	Sheffield Wednesday	Everton	2–1
1908	Wolverhampton Wanderers	Newcastle United	3–1
1909	Manchester United	Bristol City	1–0
1910	Newcastle United	Barnsley	1–1 aet (2–0 replay)
1911	Bradford City	Newcastle United	0–0 aet (1–0 replay)
1912	Barnsley West	Bromwich Albion	0–0 aet (1–0 replay)
1913	Aston Villa	Sunderland	1–0
1914	Burnley	Liverpool	1–0
1915	Sheffield United	Chelsea	3–0
1920	Aston Villa	Huddersfield Town	1–0 aet
1921	Tottenham Hotspur	Wolverhampton Wanderers	1–0
1922	Huddersfield Town	Preston North End	1–0
1923	Bolton Wanderers	West Ham United	2–0
1924	Newcastle United	Aston Villa	2–0
1925	Sheffield United	Cardiff City	1–0
1926	Bolton Wanderers	Manchester City	1–0
1927	Cardiff City	Arsenal	1–0
1928	Blackburn Rovers	Huddersfield Town	3–1
1929	Bolton Wanderers	Portsmouth	2–0
1930	Arsenal	Huddersfield Town	2–0

Year	Winner	Runners-Up	Result
1931	West Bromwich Albion	Birmingham City	2–1
1932	Newcastle United	Arsenal	2–1
1933	Everton	Manchester City	3–0
1934	Manchester City	Portsmouth	2–1
1935	Sheffield Wednesday	West Bromwich Albion	4–2
1936	Arsenal	Sheffield United	1–0
1937	Sunderland	Preston North End	3–1
1938	Preston North End	Huddersfield Town	1–0 aet
1939	Portsmouth	Wolverhampton Wanderers	4–1
1946	Derby County	Charlton Athletic	4–1 aet
1947	Charlton Athletic	Burnley	1–0 aet
1948	Manchester United	Blackpool	4–2
1949	Wolverhampton Wanderers	Leicester City	3–1
1950	Arsenal	Liverpool	2–0
1951	Newcastle United	Blackpool	2–0
1952	Newcastle United	Arsenal	1–0
1953	Blackpool	Bolton Wanderers	4–3
1954	West Bromwich Albion	Preston North End	3–2
1955	Newcastle United	Manchester City	3–1
1956	Manchester City	Birmingham City	3–1
1957	Aston Villa	Manchester United	2–1
1958	Bolton Wanderers	Manchester United	2–0
1959	Nottingham Forest	Luton Town	2–1
1960	Wolverhampton Wanderers	Blackburn Rovers	3–0
1961	Tottenham Hotspur	Leicester City	2–0

Year	Winner	Runners-Up	Result
1962	Tottenham Hotspur	Burnley	3–1
1963	Manchester United	Leicester City	3–1
1964	West Ham United	Preston North End	3–2
1965	Liverpool	Leeds United	2–1 aet
1966	Everton	Sheffield Wednesday	3–2
1967	Tottenham Hotspur	Chelsea	2–1
1968	West Bromwich	Albion Everton	1–0 aet
1969	Manchester City	Leicester City	1–0
1970	Chelsea	Leeds United	2–2 aet (2–1 replay)
1971	Arsenal	Liverpool	2–1 aet
1972	Leeds United	Arsenal	1–0
1973	Sunderland	Leeds United	1–0
1974	Liverpool	Newcastle United	3–0
1975	West Ham United	Fulham	2–0
1976	Southampton	Manchester United	1–0
1977	Manchester United	Liverpool	2–1
1978	Ipswich Town	Arsenal	1–0
1979	Arsenal	Manchester United	3–2
1980	West Ham United	Arsenal	1–0
1981	Tottenham Hotspur	Manchester City	1–1 aet (3–2 replay)
1982	Tottenham Hotspur	Queens Park Rangers	1–1 aet (1–0 replay)
1983	Manchester United	Brighton and Hove Albion	2–2 aet (4–0 replay)
1984	Everton	Watford	2–0
1985	Manchester United	Everton	1–0 aet
1986	Liverpool	Everton	3–1
1987	Coventry City	Tottenham Hotspur	3–2 aet
1988	Wimbledon	Liverpool	1–0

Year	Winner	Runners-Up	Result
1989	Liverpool	Everton	3–2 aet
1990	Manchester United	Crystal Palace	3–3 aet (1–0 replay)
1991	Tottenham Hotspur	Nottingham Forest	2–1 aet
1992	Liverpool	Sunderland	2–0
1993	Arsenal	Sheffield Wednesday	1–1 aet (2–1 replay aet)
1994	Manchester United	Chelsea	4–0
1995	Everton	Manchester United	1–0
1996	Manchester United	Liverpool	1–0
1997	Chelsea	Middlesbrough	2–0
1998	Arsenal	Newcastle United	2–0
1999	Manchester United	Newcastle United	2–0
2000	Chelsea	Aston Villa	1–0
2001	Liverpool	Arsenal	2–1
2002	Arsenal	Chelsea	2–0
2003	Arsenal	Southampton	1–0
2004	Manchester United	Millwall	3–0
2005	Arsenal	Manchester United	0–0 aet (5–4 penalty shootout)
2006	Liverpool	West Ham United	3–3 aet (3–1 penalty shootout)
2007	Chelsea	Manchester United	1–0
2008	Portsmouth	Cardiff City	1–0

British Home Championship Results

Year	Winner
1884–85	Scotland
1886	England/Scotland (shared)
1887	Scotland
1888	England
1889	Scotland
1890	Scotland/England (shared)
1891–93	England
1894	Scotland
1895	England
1896–97	Scotland
1898–99	England
1900	Scotland
1901	England
1902	Scotland
1903	England/Ireland/Scotland (shared)
1904–05	England
1906	England/Scotland (shared)
1907	Wales
1908	Scotland/England (shared)
1909	England
1910	Scotland
1911	England
1912	England/Scotland (shared)
1913	England
1914	Ireland
1915–19	Not contested due to the First World War
1920	Wales
1921–23	Scotland
1924	Wales

Year	Winner
1925–26	Scotland
1927	Scotland/England (shared)
1928	Wales
1929	Scotland
1930	England
1931	Scotland/England (shared)
1932	England
1933–34	Wales
1935	England/Scotland (shared)
1936	Scotland
1937	Wales
1938	England
1939	England/Scotland/Wales (shared)
1946	Not contested due to the Second World War
1947–48	England
1949	Scotland
1950	England
1951	Scotland
1952	Wales/England (shared)
1953	England/Scotland (shared)
1954–55	England
1956	England/Scotland/Wales/Northern Ireland (shared)
1957	England
1958	England/Northern Ireland (shared)
1959	Northern Ireland/England (shared)
1960	England/Scotland/Wales (shared)
1961	England
1962–63	Scotland
1964	Scotland/England/Northern Ireland (shared)
1965–66	England
1967	Scotland

Year	Winner
1968–69	England
1970	England/Scotland/Wales (shared)
1971	England
1972	England/Scotland (shared)
1973	England
1974	Scotland/England (shared)
1975	England
1976–77	Scotland
1978–79	England
1980	Northern Ireland
1981	Not finished
1982–83	England
1984	Northern Ireland

Scottish Cup Results Winners 1874–2008

- 34 Celtic
- 32 Rangers
- 10 Queen's Park
- 7 Aberdeen, Heart Of Midlothian
- 3 Vale Of Leven, Clyde, St. Mirren, Kilmarnock
- 2 Renton, Hibernian, Third Lanark, Falkirk,
- 1 Dunfermline Athletic, Motherwell
- 1 Dumbarton, St. Bernard's, Dundee, Partick Thistle, Morton, Airdrieonians, East Fife, Dundee United
- 1 withheld

UEFA Cup Results

Year	Winner
2008	FC Zenit St. Petersburg
2007	Sevilla FC
2006	Sevilla FC
2005	PFC CSKA Moskva
2004	Valencia CF
2003	FC Porto
2002	Feyenoord
2001	Liverpool FC
2000	Galatasaray AŞ
1999	Parma FC
1998	FC Internazionale Milano
1997	FC Schalke 04
1996	FC Bayern München
1995	Parma FC
1994	FC Internazionale Milano
1993	Juventus
1992	AFC Ajax
1991	FC Internazionale Milano
1990	Juventus
1989	SSC Napoli
1988	Bayer 04 Leverkusen
1987	IFK Göteborg
1986	Real Madrid CF
1985	Real Madrid CF
1984	Tottenham Hotspur FC
1983	RSC Anderlecht
1982	IFK Göteborg
1981	Ipswich Town FC
1980	Eintracht Frankfurt
1979	VfL Borussia Mönchengladbach

Year	Winner
1978	PSV Eindhoven
1977	Juventus
1976	Liverpool FC
1975	VfL Borussia Mönchengladbach
1974	Feyenoord
1973	Liverpool FC
1972	Tottenham Hotspur FC

UEFA Super Cup Results

Year	Winner
2007	AC Milan
2006	Sevilla FC
2005	Liverpool FC
2004	Valencia CF
2003	AC Milan
2002	Real Madrid CF
2001	Liverpool FC
2000	Galatasaray AŞ
1999	SS Lazio
1998	Chelsea FC
1997	FC Barcelona
1996	Juventus
1995	AFC Ajax
1994	AC Milan
1993	Parma FC
1992	FC Barcelona
1991	Manchester United FC
1990	AC Milan
1989	AC Milan
1988	KV Mechelen

Year	Winner
1987	FC Porto
1986	FC Steaua Bucureşti
1984	Juventus
1983	Aberdeen FC
1982	Aston Villa FC
1980	Valencia CF
1979	Nottingham Forest FC
1978	RSC Anderlecht
1977	Liverpool FC
1976	RSC Anderlecht
1975	FC Dynamo Kyiv
1973	AFC Ajax

Pan American Games

Year	Winner
1951	Argentina
1955	Argentina
1959	Argentina
1963	Brazil
1967	Mexico
1971	Argentina
1975	Brazil and Mexico (shared)
1979	Brazil
1983	Uruguay
1987	Brazil
1991	United States
1995	Argentina
1999	Mexico
2003	Argentina
2007	Ecuador

Oceania Nations Cup

Year	Winner
1973	New Zealand
1980	Australia
1996	Australia
1998	New Zealand
2000	Australia
2002	New Zealand
2004	Australia
2008	New Zealand

Gulf Cup Of Nations Results

Year	Winner
1970	Kuwait
1972	Kuwait
1974	Kuwait
1976	Kuwait
1979	Iraq
1982	Kuwait
1984	Iraq
1986	Kuwait
1988	Iraq
1990	Kuwait
1992	Qatar
1994	Saudi Arabia
1996	Kuwait
1998	Kuwait
2000	cancelled
2002	Saudi Arabia

Year	Winner
2004	Saudi Arabia
2004	Qatar
2007	United Arab Emirates
2009	Oman

Pan Arab Games

Year	Winner
1953	Egypt
1957	Syria
1961	Morocco
1965	Egypt
1976	Morocco
1985	Iraq
1992	Egypt
1997	Jordan
1999	Jordan
2007	Egypt

ARAB NATIONS CUP RESULTS

Year	Winner	Runners-Up	Venue
1963	Tunisia	Syria	Lebanon
1964	Iraq	Libya	Kuwait
1966	Iraq	Syria	Iraq
1985	Iraq	Bahrain	Saudi Arabia
1988	Iraq	Syria	Jordan
1992	Egypt (Olympic team)	Saudi Arabia	Syria
1998	Saudi Arabia	Qatar	Qatar
2002	Saudi Arabia	Bahrain	Kuwait

Canadian National Challenge Cup Winners

Year	Winner
1913–14	Norwood Wanderers of Winnipeg
1915	Winnipeg Scottish
1916–18	Not held due to First World War
1919	Montreal Grand
1920	Hamilton Westinghouse
1921	Toronto Scottish
1922	Calgary Hillhursts
1923	Naniamo Wanderers
1924	United Weston (Winnipeg)
1925	Toronto Ulster
1926	United Weston (Winnipeg)
1927	Naniamo Wanderers
1928	New Westminster Royals
1929	Montreal CNR
1930–31	New Westminster Royals
1932	Toronto Scottish Vancouver
1933	Toronto Scottish
1934	Verdun Park (Montreal)
1935	Montreal Aldrods
1936	New Westminster Royals
1937	Johnston Nationals (B.C.)
1938	Vancouver North Shore
1939	Vancouver Radials
1940–1945	not held due to Second World War
1946	Toronto Ulster United
1947	Vancouver St. Andrews
1948	Montreal Carsteel
1949	Vancouver North Shore
1950	Vancouver City

Year	Winner
1951	Toronto Ulster United
1952	Montreal Stelco
1953	New Westminster Royals
1954	Winnipeg Scottish
1955	New Westminster Royals
1956	Vancouver Halecos
1957	Montreal Ukraina
1958	New Westminster Royals
1959	Montreal Alouettes
1960	New Westminster Royals
1961	Montreal Concordia
1962	Winnipeg Scottish
1963	No competition
1964	Vancouver Columbus
1965	Vancouver Firefighters
1966	British Columbia
1967	Ballymena United (Toronto)
1968	Toronto Royals
1969	Vancouver Columbus
1970	No competition
1971	Vancouver Eintracht
1972	New Westminster Blues
1973	Vancouver Firefighters
1974	Calgary Kickers
1975	London Boxing Club
1976	Victoria west
1977–78	Vancouver Columbus
1979	Victoria West
1980	Saint John Drydock
1981	Toronto Ciociaro
1982	Victoria West

Year	Winner
1983	Vancouver Firefighters
1984	Victoria West
1985	Vancouver Croatia
1986	Hamilton Steelers
1987	Winnipeg Lucania
1988	St. John's Holy Cross
1989	Scarborough Azzuri
1990	Vancouver Firefighters
1991–92	Vancouver Norvan ANAF
1993	Vancouver Westside Rino
1994	Edmonton Ital-Canadians
1995	Mistral-Estrie
1996	Westside CIBC
1997	Edmonton Ital-Canadians
1998	RDP Condores PQ
1999	Calgary Celtics
2000	Winnipeg Lucania
2001	Halifax King of Donair
2002	Winnipeg Sons of Italy
2003	Calgary Callies
2004	Pegasus FC
2005	Scarborough GS United
2006	Ottawa St. Anthony Italia
2007–08	Calgary Callies

European Cup Finals Results

Year	Winner	Runners Up	Result
2007–08	Manchester United	Chelsea	1–1 aet (6–5 penalty shootout)
2006–07	AC Milan	Liverpool	2–1
2005–06	Barcelona	Arsenal	2–1
2004–05	Liverpool	Milan	3–3 aet (3–2 penalty shootout)
2003–04	Porto	AS Monaco	3–0
2002–03	AC Milan	Juventus	0–0 aet (3–2 penalty shootout)
2001–02	Real Madrid	Bayer 04 Leverkusen	2–1
2000–01	Bayern Munich	Valencia	1–1 aet (5–4 penalty shootout)
1999–00	Real Madrid	Valencia	3–0
1998–99	Manchester United	Bayern Munich	2–1
1997–98	Real Madrid	Juventus	1–0
1996–97	Borussia Dortmund	Juventus	3–1
1995–96	Juventus	Ajax	1–1 aet (4–2 penalty shootout)
1994–95	Ajax	AC Milan	1–0
1993–94	AC Milan	Barcelona	4–0
1992–93	Olympique de Marseille	AC Milan	1–0
1991–92	Barcelona	Sampdoria	1–0 aet
1990–91	Red Star Belgrade	Olympique de Marseille	0–0 aet (5–3 penalty shootout)
1989–90	AC Milan	Benfica	1–0
1988–89	AC Milan	Steaua Bucharest	4–0

Year	Winner	Runners Up	Result
1987–88	PSV Eindhoven	Benfica	0–0 aet (6–5 penalty shootout)
1986–87	Porto	Bayern Munich	2–1
1985–86	Steaua Bucharest	Barcelona	0–0 aet (2–0 penalty shootout)
1984–85	Juventus	Liverpool	1–0
1983–84	Liverpool	AS Roma	1–1 aet (4–2 penalty shootout)
1982–83	Hamburger SV	Juventus	1–0
1981–82	Aston Villa	Bayern Munich	1–0
1980–81	Liverpool	Real Madrid	1–0
1979–80	Nottingham Forest	Hamburger SV	1–0
1978–79	Nottingham Forest	Malmö FF	1–0
1977–78	Liverpool	Club Brugge	1–0
1976–77	Liverpool	VfL Borussia Mönchengladbach	3–1
1975–76	Bayern Munich	AS Saint-Étienne	1–0
1974–75	Bayern Munich	Leeds United	2–0
1973–74	Bayern Munich	Atlético Madrid	1–1 aet (4–0 replay)
1972–73	Ajax	Juventus	1–0
1971–72	Ajax	Internazionale	2–0
1970–71	Ajax	Panathinaikos	2–0
1969–70	Feyenoord	Celtic	2–1 aet
1968–69	AC Milan	Ajax	4–1
1967–68	Manchester United	Benfica	4–1 aet
1966–67	Celtic	Internazionale	2–1
1965–66	Real Madrid	FK Partizan	2–1
1964–65	Internazionale	Benfica	1–0
1963–64	Internazionale	Real Madrid	3–1
1962–63	AC Milan	Benfica	2–1
1961–62	Benfica	Real Madrid	5–3

Year	Winner	Runners Up	Result
1960–61	Benfica	Barcelona	3–2
1959–60	Real Madrid	Eintracht Frankfurt	7–3
1958–59	Real Madrid	Stade de Reims	
1957–58	Real Madrid	AC Milan	3–2 aet
1956–57	Real Madrid	AC Fiorentina	2–0
1955–56	Real Madrid	Stade de Reims	4–3

Men's Olympic Medals

Year	Gold	Silver	Bronze
1900	Great Britain	France	Belgium
1904	Canada		United States
1908	Great Britain	Denmark	Netherlands
1912	Great Britain	Denmark	Netherlands
1920	Belgium	Spain	Netherlands
1924	Uruguay	Switzerland	Sweden
1928	Uruguay	Argentina	Italy
1936	Italy	Austria	Norway
1948	Sweden	Yugoslavia	Denmark
1952	Hungary	Yugoslavia	Sweden
1956	USSR	Yugoslavia	Bulgaria
1960	Yugoslavia	Denmark	Hungary
1964	Hungary	Czechoslovakia	East Germany
1968	Hungary	Bulgaria	Japan
1972	Poland	Hungary	USSR
1976	East Germany	Poland	USSR
1980	Czechoslovakia	East Germany	USSR
1984	France	Brazil	Yugoslavia
1988	USSR	Brazil	West Germany
1992	Spain	Poland	Ghana
1996	Nigeria	Argentina	Brazil

Year	Gold	Silver	Bronze
2000	Cameroon	Spain	Chile
2004	Argentina	Paraguay	Italy
2008	Argentina	Nigeria	Brazil

Men's Pan American Games Medalists

Year	Gold	Silver	Bronze
1951	Argentina	Costa Rica	Chile
1955	Argentina	Mexico	Netherlands Antilles
1959	Argentina	Brazil	United States
1963	Brazil	Argentina	Chile
1967	Mexico	Bermuda	Trinidad and Tobago
1971	Argentina	Columbia	Cuba
1975	Mexico and Brazil (tie)	n/a	Argentina
1979	Brazil	Cuba	Argentina
1983	Uruguay	Guatemala	Brazil
1987	Brazil	Chile	Argentina
1991	United States	Mexico	Cuba
1995	Argentina	Mexico	Colombia
1999	Mexico	Honduras	United States
2003	Argentina	Brazil	Mexico
2007	Ecuador	Jamaica	Mexico

Copa America Finals Results

Year	Winners
1910	Argentina
1916	Uruguay
1917	Uruguay
1919	Brazil

Year	Winners
1920	Uruguay
1921	Argentina
1922	Brazil
1923	Uruguay
1924	Uruguay
1925	Argentina
1926	Uruguay
1927	Argentina
1929	Argentina
1935	Uruguay
1937	Argentina
1939	Peru
1941	Argentina
1942	Uruguay
1945	Argentina
1946	Argentina
1947	Argentina
1949	Brazil
1953	Paraguay
1955	Argentina
1957	Argentina
1958	Argentina
1959	Uruguay
1963	Bolivia
1967	Uruguay
1975	Peru
1979	Paraguay
1983	Uruguay
1987	Uruguay
1989	Brazil
1991	Argentina
1993	Argentina

Year	Winners
1995	Uruguay
1997	Brazil
1999	Brazil
2001	Colombia
2004	Brazil

Women's World Cup Finals Results

Year	Winner	Runners-Up	Result
1991	United States	Norway	2–1
1995	Norway	United States	1–0
1999	United States	China	0–0 aet (5–4 penalty shootout)
2003	Germany	Sweden	2–1
2007	Germany	Brazil	2–0

Women's Olympic Medalists

Year	Gold	Silver	Bronze
1996	United States	China	Norway
2000	Norway	United	Germany
2004	United States	Brazil	Germany
2008	United States	Brazil	Germany

Women's Pan American Games Medalists

Year	Gold	Silver	Bronze
1999	United States	Mexico	Costa Rica
2003	Brazil	Canada	Mexico
2007	Brazil	United States	Canada

Welsh Cup Finals Results

Year	Winners	Runners-Up
1877–78	Wrexham Town	Druids
1878–79	Newtown White Stars	Wrexham Town
1879–80	Druids	Ruthin
1880–81	Druids	Newtown White Stars
1881–82	Druids	Northwich Victoria
1882–83	Wrexham	Druids
1883–84	Oswestry White Stars	Druids
1884–85	Druids	Oswestry White Stars
1885–86	Druids	Newtown
1886–87	Chirk	Davenham
1887–88	Chirk	Newtown
1888–89	Bangor	Northwich Victoria
1889–90	Chirk	Wrexham
1890–91	Shrewsbury Town	Wrexham
1891–92	Chirk	Westminster Rovers
1892–93	Wrexham	Chirk
1893–94	Chirk	Westminster Rovers
1894–95	Newtown	Wrexham
1895–96	Bangor	Wrexham
1896–97	Wrexham	Newtown
1897–98	Druids	Wrexham
1898–99	Druids	Wrexham
1899–1900	Aberystwyth	Druids
1900–01	Oswestry United	Druids
1901–02	Wellington Town	Wrexham
1902–03	Wrexham	Aberaman Athletic
1903–04	Druids	Aberdare Athletic
1904–05	Wrexham	Aberdare Athletic
1905–06	Wellington Town	Whitchurch
1906–07	Oswestry United	Whitchurch

Year	Winners	Runners-Up
1907–08	Chester	Connah's Quay and Shotton
1908–09	Wrexham	Chester
1909–10	Wrexham	Chester
1910–11	Wrexham	Connah's Quay and Shotton
1911–12	Cardiff City	Pontypridd
1912–13	Swansea Town	Pontypridd
1913–14	Wrexham	Llanelli
1914–15	Wrexham	Swansea Town
1915–19	No Competition Held	
1919–20	Cardiff City	Wrexham
1920–21	Wrexham	Pontypridd
1921–22	Cardiff City	Ton Pentre
1922–23	Cardiff City	Aberdare Athletic
1923–24	Wrexham	Merthyr Tydfil
1924–25	Wrexham	Fflint
1925–26	Ebbw Vale	Swansea Town
1926–27	Cardiff City	Rhyl
1927–28	Cardiff City	Bangor City
1928–29	Connah's Quay and Shotton	Cardiff City
1929–30	Cardiff City	Rhyl
1930–31	Wrexham	Shrewsbury Town
1931–32	Swansea Town	Wrexham
1932–33	Chester	Wrexham
1933–34	Bristol City	Tranmere Rovers
1934–35	Tranmere Rovers	Chester
1935–36	Crewe Alexandra	Chester
1936–37	Crewe Alexandra	Rhyl
1937–38	Shrewsbury Town	Swansea Town
1938–39	South Liverpool	Cardiff City
1939–40	Wellington Town	Swansea Town
1940–46	No Competition Held	
1946–47	Chester	Merthyr Tydfil

Year	Winners	Runners-Up
1947–48	Lovell's Athletic	Shrewsbury Town
1948–49	Merthyr Tydfil	Swansea Town
1949–50	Swansea Town	Wrexham
1950–51	Merthyr Tydfil	Cardiff City
1951–52	Rhyl	Merthyr Tydfil
1952–53	Rhyl	Chester
1953–54	Fflint Town United	Chester
1954–55	Barry Town	Chester
1955–56	Cardiff City	Swansea Town
1956–57	Wrexham	Swansea Town
1957–58	Wrexham	Chester
1958–59	Cardiff City	Lovell's Athletic
1959–60	Wrexham	Cardiff City
1960–61	Swansea Town	Bangor City
1961–62	Bangor City	Wrexham
1962–63	Borough United	Newport County
1963–64	Cardiff City	Bangor City
1964–65	Cardiff City	Wrexham
1965–66	Swansea Town	Chester
1966–67	Cardiff City	Wrexham
1967–68	Cardiff City	Hereford United
1968–69	Cardiff City	Swansea Town
1969–70	Cardiff City	Chester
1970–71	Cardiff City	Wrexham
1971–72	Wrexham	Cardiff City
1972–73	Cardiff City	Bangor City
1973–74	Cardiff City	Stourbridge
1974–75	Wrexham	Cardiff City
1975–76	Cardiff City	Hereford United
1976–77	Shrewsbury Town	Cardiff City
1977–78	Wrexham	Bangor City

Year	Winners	Runners-Up
1978–79	Shrewsbury Town	Wrexham
1979–80	Newport County	Shrewsbury Town
1980–81	Swansea City	Hereford United
1981–82	Swansea City	Cardiff City
1982–83	Swansea City	Wrexham
1983–84	Shrewsbury Town	Wrexham
1984–85	Shrewsbury Town	Bangor City
1985–86	Wrexham	Kidderminster Harriers
1986–87	Merthyr Tydfil	Newport County
1987–88	Cardiff City	Wrexham
1988–89	Swansea City	Kidderminster Harriers
1989–90	Hereford United	Wrexham
1990–91	Swansea City	Wrexham
1991–92	Cardiff City	Hednesford Town
1992–93	Cardiff City	Rhyl
1993–94	Barry Town	Cardiff City
1994–95	Wrexham	Cardiff City
1995–96	Llansantffraid	Barry Town
1996–97	Barry Town	Cwmbran Town
1997–98	Bangor City	Connah's Quay Nomads
1998–99	ICT Cardiff	Carmarthen Town
1999–00	Bangor City	Cwmbran Town
2000–01	Barry Town	Total Network Solutions FC
2001–02	Barry Town	Bangor City
2002–03	Barry Town	Cwmbran Town
2003–04	Rhyl	Total Network Solutions FC
2004–05	Total Network Solutions FC	Carmarthen Town
2005–06	Rhyl	Bangor City
2006–07	Carmarthen Town	Afan Lido
2007–08	Bangor City	Lianelli

Other Books in the Now You Know Series

**Now You Know
Hockey**
978-1-55002-869-0
$19.99

**Now You Know
Golf**
978-1-55002-870-6
$19.99

**Now You Know
Football**
978-1-55488-453-7
$19.99

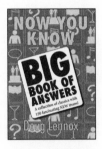

**Now You Know
Big Book of Sports**
978-1-55488-454-4
$29.99

**Now You Know
Big Book of Answers**
978-1-55002-741-9
$29.99, US$26.99

**Now You Know
Big Book of Answers 2**
978-1-55002-871-3
$29.99

More Books in the Now You Know Series

Available at your favourite bookseller.

DUNDURN PRESS
www.dundurn.com

Did Now You Know satiate your desire for little-known facts, or do you want more? Visit www.nowyouknowitall.com and sign up for the Answer of the Week and have a little-known fact delivered straight into your inbox!